A Guide to Making Money Through Environment-Friendly Stocks

Green investing

SECOND EDITION

JACK ULDRICH

author of *The Next Big Thing Is Really Small*

Aadamsmedia

Avon, Massachusetts

Copyright © 2010, 2008 by Jack Uldrich
All rights reserved.
This book, or parts thereof, may not be reproduced in any
form without permission from the publisher; exceptions are
made for brief excerpts used in published reviews.

Published by
Adams Media, a division of F+W Media, Inc.
57 Littlefield Street, Avon, MA 02322
www.adamsmedia.com

ISBN 10: 1-4405-0374-5
ISBN 13: 978-1-4405-0374-0

Printed in the United States.

10 9 8 7 6 5 4 3 2 1

Library of Congress Cataloging-in-Publication Data
is available from the publisher.

This publication is designed to provide accurate and authoritative information
with regard to the subject matter covered. It is sold with the understanding
that the publisher is not engaged in rendering legal, accounting, or other
professional advice. If legal advice or other expert assistance is required, the
services of a competent professional person should be sought.
—From a *Declaration of Principles* jointly adopted by a Committee of the
American Bar Association and a Committee of Publishers and Associations

Many of the designations used by manufacturers and sellers to distinguish
their product are claimed as trademarks. Where those designations appear in
this book and Adams Media was aware of a trademark claim, the designations
have been printed with initial capital letters.

This book is available at quantity discounts for bulk purchases.
For information, please call 1-800-289-0963.

The Sustainable Forestry Initiative® program
promotes responsible environmental
behavior and sound forest management.

Contents

Editor's Note

Different people use different terms to refer to investing in renewable energy companies. Some refer to it as green or greentech investing, while others label it cleantech investing—because the energy sources are nonpolluting, hence clean. For the purposes of this book, the various terms are interchangeable. They will be used to describe companies that employ innovative technologies to create new products, processes, and services that compete favorably with existing energy sources, technologies, and services in terms of price and performance, while simultaneously reducing mankind's impact on the environment.

The terms *cleantech* and *green tech* will primarily be used to describe companies seeking to generate energy from alternative energy sources, including sun, wind, biofuels, geothermal, fuel cell technology, and wave power. Some attention will also be devoted to companies developing more resource-efficient industrial processes that help conserve energy usage and/or reduce harmful environmental emissions.

It is worth noting that as of 2009 there were an estimated 900 companies that could be legitimately classified as cleantech companies. In the interest of both time and space, this book has focused on eighty-five of the most promising companies participating in the green tech arena. Obviously, the list is somewhat subjective, but every effort has been made to discern those companies likely to have the biggest impact in the energy sector.

Furthermore, because this is a book on investing, more attention has been paid to publicly traded cleantech companies than to privately owned ones. The private companies profiled were selected either because they may soon be publicly traded or, alternatively, their technology was deemed capable of "disrupting" an existing market (i.e., taking a significant amount of market share away from a particular source of energy) and thus might represent a significant economic threat to an existing publicly traded energy company or even an entire industry.

"We are going to see a better market emerge for cleantech . . . looking to the next 12 to 24 months there is a huge opportunity moving forward."
—Nicholas Parker, Executive Chairman of the Cleantech Group, January 2009

"We will double our capacity to generate alternative sources of energy like wind, solar, and biofuels over the next three years."
—President Barack Obama, February 17, 2009

Chapter One

Green Investing: It's All about the Green—Money

After a blockbuster year in 2007, 2008 and the first half of 2009 were difficult for investors in clean technology. The average mutual fund or exchange-traded fund concentrating in the area was down 50 percent, and dozens of businesses were forced into bankruptcy. Scores more were brought to the edge of insolvency. The good news, if you will, was that clean technology wasn't alone in feeling the wrath of this collapse. The entire Dow Jones Index fell from a high of 14,000 to less than 8,000. The cause was the near total meltdown of the global financial markets.

The silver lining in this otherwise gloomy situation is that many cleantech companies' valuations are now significantly discounted from their recent historic highs. This does not mean that "screaming deals" abound (as you will see from the profiles of many of the companies), but a series of factors are creating favorable headwinds, and this is an excellent time to consider investments in the sector.

First, there is that most valuable of all factors—money. In 2008, in spite of the global financial crisis, cleantech was still able to bring in $155 billion in investments worldwide. This is quadruple the amount of four years earlier, and it suggests bankers, investors, and venture capitalists still see promise in the sector in spite of the economic climate. The majority of this money went to finance existing projects, but venture capital was also up 38 percent to $8.4 billion.

The lesson for investors in these numbers is that at least in the short term the environment will favor existing, larger companies over smaller start-ups. The latter may have impressive or promising technology, but if they can't get financing they are unlikely to go anywhere. The fact that venture capitalists are still aggressively investing in the sector suggests there is no shortage of promising companies lurking on the horizon. Many of these companies will be profiled in the pages ahead.

The second macroeconomic factor working in the industry's favor is the growing and unparalleled support for clean technology from governments around the world. As one industry analyst said, "As long as there is government support for clean energy, the future of the industry is assured." Normally (and philosophically) I'm not a proponent of government support for industries and am wary of any field that is overly reliant on the largesse of politicians and bureaucrats; but, in the case of cleantech, early government support will provide a critical bridge to many of these industries until their energy sources become price-competitive with conventional fossil fuels. In the case of wind and solar power, this "grid parity" may be achieved as early as 2012.

The size and scope of this governmental support is not to be underestimated. In February of 2009, President Obama signed the American Recovery and Reinvestment Act. Of the total $787 billion in the stimulus package, an estimated $30 billion is directed toward clean energy. China is also investing $30 billion of its $586 billion economic stimulus, and South Korea is going further still by investing $38 billion.

Governmental support is not just limited to cash, tax credits, and grants for wind, solar power, biofuels, smart grid, and energy efficiency; legislators and regulators are soon expected to level the playing field in favor of renewable energy sources— at the expense of carbon-based fuels. In California, the governor signed an executive order increasing to 33 percent (from 20 percent) the amount of energy utilities must derive from renewable sources by 2020. Similar action by the federal government will soon follow. Elsewhere, ten Northeastern states have now enacted a market for carbon trading. Like California's renewable energy standard, this is also a harbinger of federal action. The U.S. Congress also plans to enact a cap-and-trade system. Such legislation will put a tangible price on the emissions of carbon-based fossil fuels. The net effect will be that renewable energy will become more affordable *vis-à-vis* coal, oil, and natural gas. (An even bigger whammy could come in December 2009, if the United Nations conference in Copenhagen is able to reach a meaningful agreement on the global regulation of carbon.)

The influx of this private and public money in combination with the distinct possibility of market-altering legislation and regulation points toward long-term growth. As do a series of other factors.

A Long-Term Secular Trend

A few years ago, two separate research organizations published comprehensive reports on cleantech. The first, by Cleantech Venture Network, noted that the amount of energy produced from alternative, renewable sources was expected to grow at near exponential rates for the next decade. Wind power, for instance, the report said, would triple from $17 billion to $60 billion in 2016; biofuels would increase four times from $20 billion to $80 billion in the same period; solar would spike from $15 billion to $70 billion; and even fuel cell technology will experience an elevenfold increase from $1.4 billion to $16 billion within a decade's time.

The second firm, Lux Research, didn't publicly release its projections but did note that the growth of energy produced from alternative, renewable energy sources was a "long-term secular trend." Since the publication of the first edition of this book in the spring of 2008, this scenario has been borne out. Both wind and solar have demonstrated impressive growth; and, from 2009 to 2012, wind capacity is expected to grow another 160 percent to a total of 268,000 MegaWatts (MW), while solar is estimated to grow by 350 percent to 72,000 MW. Five factors are fueling this growth.

First, in spite of recently declining oil prices, most experts now agree that oil is a dwindling natural resource and finding and delivering new oil will continue to get more costly. To the extent that the price does go up, alternative energies will continue to become more attractive.

In the summer of 2009, the price of a barrel of oil was $70 and gas hovered between $2.50 and $3.00 a gallon. This is significant not because it is an indication that the price will continue to go up, but rather because at this price it makes sense for companies to begin investing in the development of alternative energies. Many alternative energy projects make little to no financial sense when oil is below $50 a barrel but suddenly become practical above that price. Once the rationale is there, large investments are made in these energy sources. And once these upfront investments have been made, there is little or no incentive to discontinue production even if the price of oil returns to more historical norms. In other words, cleantech is set on a course for which there is no reason to turn back.

The second driver of clean energy will be the overall increase in global demand for energy. Today, over 6 billion people populate the planet. By 2050, the number is expected to surge to 9 billion.

At the same time the countries with the fasting-growing populations—China and India—are adding to their population, they are also growing in economic terms at an astronomical rate. The combination of economic and population pressure is placing an unprecedented strain on traditional energy sources. As the law of supply and demand adjusts to newer, higher price equilibrium, it will work to the advantage of those clean energy sources that are abundant, such as solar, wind, and geothermal.

To put the issue in some perspective: between 2000 and 2008, China's oil consumption increased 7 percent annually, and it is expected to maintain this level of growth through 2017. What this means is that between 2009 and 2017, the country's total oil consumption will nearly double. This kind of demand could leave Americans pining for the days when gas was "only" $3.00 a gallon.

Depending on what energy sources the developing world uses, the environmental costs could also skyrocket. In China alone, the country expects to build the equivalent of one new coal plant every week for the next decade in order to meet its nearly insatiable demand for electricity. If true, the country, which has now surpassed the United States as the world's largest contributor of carbon dioxide, could easily negate even the best efforts by the other world nations to limit and cut back on their carbon emissions.

To this end, the public's growing awareness of climate change is the third driver of cleantech as a long-term secular trend. From the fate of polar bears facing the melting of their habitat in the Arctic to coral reefs withering off the coast of Australia, governments around the world appeared poised to finally address the issue. As stated earlier, the UN conference in December 2009 in Copenhagen will be a good barometer.

The fourth and fifth drivers of cleantech go hand in hand. As already explained, an extraordinary amount of money is being invested in clean energy technologies by governments, large corporations, and venture capitalists, and this money is fueling the creation and development of a variety of very promising technologies. Of course, it is not the money itself that truly matters but rather what that money is used for.

Many of the innovations will be documented in the pages ahead, but to get a sense of what the money has so far meant to the burgeoning industry, it is helpful to consider that 3,000 new cleantech patents were filed in 2008. This number is expected to double again by the end of the decade. Now, not all of these patents matter, but even if just a few do they could, quite literally, change the world—and therein lies the real opportunity for cleantech and green investing.

While it is impossible to precisely predict how cleantech will affect the world's energy options in the years ahead, it would be naive to think that new wind turbine designs; advances in the efficiency of solar cells and battery technology; as well as progress in fields as varied as fuel cell, wave power, and synthetic biology won't change the competitive landscape of the energy industry.

It seems increasingly clear that much of the energy the world needs is already here—shining down on us in the form of sunlight, blowing in the wind, growing on farmland in the form of biomass, pulsating back and forth with the oceans' tides in the form of wave power, and maybe even hovering just below the surface of the earth in the form of geothermal energy.

If so, cleantech could, as John Doerr said, be the "largest economic opportunity of the twenty-first century."

Dangers

In the last edition of this book I wrote that "if you are considering investing in cleantech in the hopes of retiring a millionaire [soon], then this book is not for you." I stand by those words.

This is not to say cleantech won't be a huge and growing field. It will. Rather, my point is to temper "irrational exuberance." More important, I want to remind investors that just because a field will be big does not mean every company or even a majority of the companies playing in that space will be successful. They won't.

Benjamin Graham, in his classic best-selling book *The Intelligent Investor*, which has been praised by no less an authority on investing than the legendary Warren Buffet as being "the best book on investing ever written," began with a variation on this warning.

He wrote: "It has long been the prevalent view that the art of successful investing lies first in the choice of those industries that are most likely to grow in the future and then in identifying the most promising companies in those industries." Graham went on to add in the first edition of his book (written in 1949), that "such an investor may for example be a buyer of air-transport stocks because he believes their future is even more brilliant than the trend the market already reflects" and "because it was fairly easy to forecast that the volume of air traffic would grow spectacularly over the years."

Not surprisingly, history has borne out Mr. Graham's first investing "moral": "Obvious prospects for physical growth in a business do not translate into obvious profits for investors." For example, it is now commonly accepted that the cumulative earnings of the airline industry over its entire history have been negative. That is, since the Wright Brothers first achieved flight in December of 1903, the airline industry has been a net *loser* of money. A number of issues contributed to this shameful state of the industry—technological problems, intense competition, overcapacity, a host of managerial, regulatory, and labor-related problems, and, more recently, problems associated with the tragic events of 9/11. However singular the example, it serves as a reminder that any industry can grow rapidly and even become a vital part of the economy but still lose money.

Now, I don't believe cleantech will be a net loser of money, but with this little historical lesson in mind, my first piece of advice is that investors should limit the portion of their portfolio invested in cleantech to a maximum of between 5 and 10 percent.

Second, the historical analogy to the airline industry is appropriate.

For starters, as in the early aviation industry, any number of clean-energy technologies are likely to encounter unexpected problems. For instance, some techniques, such as efficiently converting cellulosic feedstocks into ethanol, may take longer than expected to achieve, or other technologies, such as safe, affordable hydrogen fuel cells or reliable wave power machines, may ultimately prove impractical. It is possible, too, that most clean-energies will work exactly as promised but one specific technology will prove to be "first among equals" and render other clean energy technologies obsolete, impractical, or uncompetitive.

A third warning is that change rarely happens as fast as people expect. Almost every industry, regardless of its unique characteristics, goes through cycles of hype and troughs of despair. A more recent analogy is the Internet. In 1999, most Internet companies could do no wrong. By 2001, most of the funding had dried up, and even solid companies with legitimate business models were struggling. The wild fluctuation in the cleantech stocks—from their soaring highs in early 2008 to their bruising lows in early 2009—are reminiscent of this all-too-common trend.

For all of these reasons, it will be essential that investors continue to do due diligence on the companies profiled in this book. Chapter 2 will provide an overview of how to do this. It will also be important to diversify one's portfolio with a mix of small and large companies. Chapter 3 will focus exclusively on the largest cleantech companies. Chapters 4 through 9 will cover biofuels, solar power, wind power, "alternative" energy, and energy efficiency sectors, respectively. The book will conclude with a list of valuable cleantech resources; an overview of some of the leading clean-energy mutual funds and exchange-traded funds; and a sample portfolio, which the reader may wish to consult when putting together his or her green investing portfolio.

"Fortune favors the prepared mind."

—Louis Pasteur

Chapter Two

Due Diligence: Do Your Homework

Among the other associated dangers of placing a portion of one's money in an emerging field such as clean technology is that, by its nature, many of the companies in the industry do not have a track record by which to evaluate those organizations using traditional valuation methodologies. For instance, many cleantech companies are still in the "pre-revenue" stage, meaning that they are not yet generating any revenue. Others have either untested technologies or are investing a good deal of money developing the technologies. The latter often results in companies that have very high cash burn rates. The implication for early investors is that if a company burns through all of its money before it has a workable technology, it could go bankrupt; or it will have to go back to investors to raise additional money, which will dilute one's original investment.

Other dangers that are lurking in the cleantech waters include the considerable competition in the field. This competition takes three forms. First, every renewable energy company is first competing against existing energy sources—oil and gas, coal, and nuclear—which have a number of advantages. For starters, they still have the advantage over renewable energy sources in terms of costs (provided one does not attempt to calculate the environmental costs). They are also large and established. As such, they have deep pockets and strong political connections and are unlikely to readily cede market share to cleantech companies.

The second form of competition will take place among other renewable energy sources. For example, corn-based ethanol will not only compete against gasoline, it will also go head-to-head with biodiesel and butanol. The same may be true of solar cell technology competing directly with fuel cell technology, and wind power vying with wave power for the attention of electric utilities.

Lastly, there is the direct competition with each field. Not all ethanol companies are equal. Corn-based ethanol companies will be competing with cellulosic-based ethanol producers, and silicon-based solar cell companies will go head-to-head with thin-film solar cell companies.

What this means is that investors will need to do their due diligence before investing in the field and then investing in individual companies. What follows is a list of practical steps that can and should be followed prior to investing in the field.

Strip the *Cleantech* Label

The first step any individual investor needs to take when conducting due diligence is to strip the term *cleantech* off whatever the company is doing and investigate it from a standard business perspective. The general rule of thumb is to invest in good business opportunities, not in broad categories such as renewable energy. Too many companies use the term loosely for investors to take any company's word at face value.

Next, a good many problems can be avoided by finding answers to the following questions:

1. Does the company talk about specific market applications for its technology or just large markets? *Beware of any company that throws around big numbers and claims its products will capture a sizeable share of any multibillion-dollar industry.* It will also be helpful to understand how its product will marketed and sold and to know whether the company has access to foreign markets.

2. How has the company's product evolved over time? If it is an ethanol company, is the company looking at producing ethanol from feedstocks other than corn? Or if it is a silicon solar company, does it have a plan or is it investing in thin-film solar technology?

3. Is the company able to subcategorize the specific market it intends to enter? Companies that claim to be a broad-based cleantech company with products and technologies appealing to a wide range of markets need to be treated with suspicion.

4. Does the company talk about product development within a reasonable time frame? Better yet, has it actually produced a real product? Companies that are only in the concept or development stage are probably still too early for the average individual investor to invest his money.

5. How does the company's technology stack up in terms of price and performance with others in the field? For instance, in the solar cell field it is important to understand that if a company is producing silicon-based solar cells it should have a long-term contract with a silicon producer to ensure a reliable supply. If a company doesn't have such a contract, it could be vulnerable to fluctuations in the price of silicon.

6. Finally, does the company have strategic partners or actual customers? Many of the markets that cleantech-enabled solutions will find a home in—biofuels, wind, solar, etc.— are large and complex. As such they are difficult for small companies to successfully enter alone. Having a strategic partner is often best, easiest, and fastest way to commercial success.

In addition to these questions, there are other factors individual investors should take into consideration. You can think of these factors as people, markets, technology, and finances. The questions to consider are as follows:

➤ Does the company have a reputable and experienced management team?

➤ Can its product or technology be mass-produced quickly, cheaply, and reliably?

➤ Does the company possess technical leadership in its field, and does it have propriety intellectual property?

➤ Does it have the financial resources to accomplish its strategic goals?

It All Starts with People

Obviously, it is not wise to focus on just one of these four factors. You have to view them as part of a whole picture. However, when beginning your due diligence, a lot of time can be saved by researching the quality of the management team. The quality of a company's management has the highest correlation to whether it succeeds or fails. An innovative or "cool" technology is not enough to guarantee success. An experienced CEO is often necessary to drive the right technology solution to the largest market. Furthermore, because it is rare that any technology—or business—ever evolves according to plan, an executive team that has actual experience growing a business is a definitive advantage. Often, these executives have learned from past mistakes and will have developed the capacity to adapt to rapidly changing environments.

A number of cleantech companies are started by scientists. Investors should not be lulled into believing that their scientific credentials alone provide them the skills to run a company. These scientists are often brilliant and understand their technology better than anyone else. They are not, however, managers or executives. Scientists don't always understand the marketplace. Moreover, they aren't trained to take risks—scientists are taught to be methodical. The latter trait is a necessary ingredient in science, but it can be deadly in business—especially in a business environment that is changing as rapidly and radically as renewable energy. Good executives know when to act, and they need to do so with less-than-perfect information.

Potential investors are encouraged to review the scientific advisory board the company has assembled. Does it have the depth and breadth of experience to really direct the company?

And are the advisors really part of the management team or are they only "paper-only" members? The more engaged these advisors are in the company—the better.

It's the Product, Stupid

Back in the 1930s, it was demonstrated that a new keyboard, called the Dvorak system, was superior to today's common QWERTY keyboard. It allowed skilled typists to type an average of 165 words per minute versus 131 words on the QWERTY system. It did this by rearranging the letters so that there was less left hand use, fewer row-to-row hops, and none of those bothersome pinky stretches.

As history has vividly demonstrated, the Dvorak system, in spite of its superiority, didn't win in the marketplace. The reason is because it required people to learn an entirely new system of typing. And while it would undoubtedly have been more efficient for those doing a lot of typing, for most users the benefits of changing to the new technology did not justify the upfront investment in time to learn a new system that would yield only a modest increase in efficiency.

The moral of this little story is just because a new technology is better, it does not guarantee that it will win in the marketplace. It also serves as a cautionary tale about the difficulty of assessing whether a market will embrace a new technology. Normally, if you told a consumer or a company that a product would yield a 20 percent increase in efficiency, they'd jump at it. Such is not the case if it requires the consumer to change behavior.

This is relevant for a variety of renewable energy sources. Some biofuels, for example, will require producers to find new methods of distributing the fuel because they are incompatible with existing systems. Additionally ethanol, biodiesel, or, longer-term, hydrogen will also require retailers to install new fueling stations, and many might balk at the high cost of installing the system, especially if the payback isn't immediate. The net effect could be that biofuels are not accepted into the commercial marketplace as quickly as proponents predict.

To help determine whether a technology has "legs," investors should be able to answer the following questions: Does the product solve a real problem for its customers? For instance, does it save its users time, money, or provide them with a benefit or freedom they didn't previously enjoy? If the product meets a real need, then investors have something worth considering. If not, investors should consider leaving it for others to fund.

Is It an Idea, a Demo, or a Real Product?

The third step in considering an investment is to discern where in the development stage the company's product is. For example, is it in the concept, preproduction, or postproduction stage? If it hasn't matured to the point where it is past the concept and an actual prototype has been developed, it is too early for most investors.

If a company's technology or product is past the concept stage, the next question investors need to consider is whether the company has demonstrated "scalability and reliability." Can its biofuel, solar cell, or wind turbine be manufactured in the quantities and sizes necessary to attract the attention of major customers? And can those products be made in a manner consistent enough to guarantee quality and performance? A number of companies have recently begun producing wind turbines that have a host of amazing properties, including high strength-to-weight ratio. As a result, their deployment is being explored by a number of large electrical utility companies, but until all of the bugs can be worked out and until the customers can be guaranteed the turbines are reliable and low maintenance, some of the turbines will remain a question mark.

The most promising sign that a cleantech company is on the verge of creating a viable business—at least in the short term—is if its technology does not require manufacturers to change any of its existing equipment or processes. As was stated earlier, it is human nature to resist change, and large companies are no different. Those companies that create technologies that don't require manufacturers to change are going to have a leg up, at least in the short term. An example of this includes those companies seeking to make coal-burning plants cleaner today. Whether a company is using nanocatalysts to neutralize nitrogen oxide or using algae to capture carbon dioxide, if a coal-burning plant doesn't have to change any of its existing technology or processes, the company has a better chance of succeeding in the commercial marketplace.

Regardless of where the product is in the development stage, investors should determine whether the company has done its homework regarding how it's going to approach the marketplace. Does the company demonstrate pricing logic? Has it determined why a customer would be willing to pay a specific price? Has it targeted specific customers? Better yet, does it already have customers?

One Is the Loneliest Number

Because many cleantech start-ups are small, they will need assistance in getting their product to market. For this they will often need partners. Therefore, at a minimum, investors should know whether a company has successfully entered into arrangements with large corporate partners who will either use their products or help produce their products. For instance, Synthetic Genomics announced that BP was investing in the company. In addition to providing the start-up a substantial amount of working capital, the partnership also offers Synthetic Genomics the potential to quickly distribute and market its product into the commercial marketplace much faster than if it was a stand-alone company.

Another company that has established a useful partnership is Metabolix, which, in mid-2007, announced that it would be partnering with Archer Daniel Midlands to produce and manufacture a biodegradable plastic. The partnership doesn't guarantee Metabolix's success, but by being able to take advantage of ADM's expertise, brand recognition, and key relationships in the consumer products industry, the company is better positioned to succeed. More recently still, battery manufacturer A123 Systems has partnered with Chrysler to supply it with lithium batteries for its new electric vehicles.

Beware of Competing Technologies . . . and Lawyers

As the two earlier sections on people and markets demonstrate, investors cannot rely on superior technology alone to drive a company's stock upward. Having said this, technology is still obviously important, and assessing a company's technology— and the intellectual property behind it—is among the most difficult and time-consuming tasks.

Certain cleantechnologies are incredibly complex and require a broad base of scientific knowledge. Some require a deep understanding of many different fields of science—biology, physics, chemistry, material sciences, and the computational sciences. Assessing the relative merits of these technologies is usually beyond the skill set of the average (or even professional) investor.

How then do you go about it? The most important thing to understand is what other technologies (and companies) are out there trying to address the same problem. For instance, Chapter 4 lists numerous companies seeking to effectively and efficiently produce ethanol from feedstocks other than corn; Chapter 5 lists a host of companies manufacturing next-generation wind turbines; and Chapter 6 documents a handful of companies developing flexible solar cells. The best advice is to beware of these competitors and then let the companies themselves explain why their technologies are superior.

Investors should not be overly impressed with the number of patents a company has. All patents do is exclude others from practicing the invention. A patent does not stop someone from creating a different way to address or solve the same problem. One company can hold 250 worthless patents, while another can possess just one very valuable patent.

The rub, of course, lies in distinguishing a worthless patent from a valuable one. Recognizing that this skill is also beyond the capability of most people—at least in a field like cleantech—investors are encouraged to look at the scientific credentials of the founder's of the company and its scientific advisory board. This is by no means a perfect measure, but to the extent that the individuals associated with the company have published papers in credible, peer-reviewed scientific journals or have established relationships with credible academic institutions, government laboratories, or corporations, it is a positive sign.

For instance, the fact that Craig Ventor, the scientist most credited with sequencing the human genome, is the founder of Synthetic Genomics doesn't necessarily guarantee his patents or related technology relating to the creation of "designer bacteria" (which can cheaply and easily produce ethanol or hydrogen) will succeed, but it does improve the odds the company's technology is on solid ground.

Investors will also want to take into consideration whether the smaller cleantech companies are partnering with large corporate companies or have received investments from leading venture capital firms. The reason is because both have scientists and trained technical advisors with the requisite skills to more thoroughly evaluate a company's technology and its intellectual property. All things being equal, if established companies and venture capital firms have assessed the technology and decided to invest in the company it is a positive sign. For example, Vinod Khosla, one of America's leading venture capitalists, has invested in Mascoma, Iogen, and Cilion (among others). Again, this doesn't guarantee that any of these companies will win in the commercial marketplace, but it does imply that each company's technology is sufficiently promising to warrant an investment.

The tactic essentially amounts to letting others do your due diligence for you, but unless one has the technical skills and the time, it is often the best that can be done. Chapter 8 lists a few of the venture capital firms that have developed some expertise in cleantech, and in the company profiles in the proceeding chapters every attempt has been made to list which venture capital firms and large companies have invested in a given company or are partnering with the company. The information should be considered a proxy for the viability of a company's technology.

Such measures are imperfect but they pale in comparison to the difficulty of assessing intellectual property. Furthermore, it is almost a given that any successful technology will draw some type of legal challenge and that this challenge will come only after time, money, and a great deal of effort have already been invested into getting the technology to the marketplace.

The best way to assess a company's position in this regard is to determine if the company itself has done its own due diligence on its intellectual property. Questions to ask are:

> Has the company thoroughly analyzed its own IP claims?
> Has it analyzed the patents held by its competitors?
> Does it have international patent protection?
> Does it have systems in place to protect its IP?

If a company has licensed its intellectual property to others, investors should understand:

> The terms and conditions of the license. Is it an exclusive, nonexclusive, or field-of-use exclusive license?
> What is the duration of the license?
> How is the patent holder compensated—in cash, equity, royalties, or some combination thereof?
> If there is a challenge, who is responsible for paying the patent prosecution costs?

As with the assessment of the technology itself, assessing such legal issues is best left to the experts—in this case the lawyers. Because such expertise is beyond the knowledge of the average investor, we are again left with the situation of relying on the legal experts of the company, partnering companies, or the venture capitalists.

Often, the best an investor can do is ask the questions, and if the answers are not satisfactory or if there are too many unanswered questions and it appears a legal challenge could either delay or entirely stop the successful introduction of the technology, it is best to hold off on an investment until such issues are resolved.

Many companies, even private companies, often have a staff person devoted to investor relations. Investors are encouraged to contact these individuals and get answers to the above questions.

Follow the Money

In real estate, realtors are fond of saying that the three most important things are location, location, and location. Some in the investment field have parroted this line and said that the three most important things for any new business are money, money, and money.

Money is obviously an important component of any business, and no business can succeed without it. For established businesses, profits are an absolute necessity over the long run. But for start-ups the situation is a little more complex.

It is unwise to give excessive attention to how much money a new private start-up has raised. For one thing, a lot of money can be a bad thing, resulting in an undisciplined business atmosphere where company executives and employees don't feel a need to squeeze out every efficiency. It may also allow company executives in the short- to midterm to cover over— and hide from investors—some fundamental problems.

When conducting due diligence on start-ups, there are a few key factors you should consider. The first is to remember that it is unwise to fund a research project. More simply put, you should only consider investing in those companies that have moved beyond the "idea" stage and are actually manufacturing—or are close to manufacturing—products. And, as was said earlier, the manufacturing process should be mature enough that products can be built on a reliable, cost-effective, and scalable basis.

A perfect example of this is Magenn, an early stage development company that is seeking to develop a high-altitude wind power system. At this stage, it is an intriguing idea, but the company has no working prototype and very little cash on hand. Obviously, such a venture is far too risky for the prudent individual investor.

The second thing to look for is something called the *skin game*. Do the company founders have their own money invested in the company? Even more important perhaps is whether they have convinced their family and friends to invest in their company. If the answer is "yes" to both questions, it is a positive sign. It speaks to the founder's confidence in the company, and it provides him a stronger incentive to succeed—no one likes to let down his family or friends.

The third factor to look for is government money. Investors should not fund research or concept-stage projects, but governments should—and often do. Therefore, consider whether a company has received grants from the Department of Energy or NASA. For example, many of the biofuel companies listed in Chapter 4 have received some government funding. In fact, a few have received very sizeable grants. For instance, Poet has received up to an $80 million grant from the Department of Energy to fund the development of a process to produce cellulosic ethanol; Konarka, a private start-up, has received multimillion dollar grants from various U.S. military departments to employ nanoscale materials in the development of flexible plastic solar cells.

The point here is not to imply that the government has an impressive track record at picking winning technologies (it doesn't), rather it is to highlight the fact that the government is, in essence, helping to underwrite a company's research and development—and it is doing it in a way that doesn't dilute investor equity. (The government doesn't ask for a stake in the company—only the right to use the technology if and when it is developed.)

Investors should, however, be cautious of companies that are either entirely reliant on government grants or who after years of government funding are unable to attract any corporate attention.

I also encourage you to consider the amount of venture capital funding a company has received. This is a dual-edge sword. On the positive side of the ledger is the fact that these firms have done their own due diligence and have found enough promise in the company to warrant a follow-on investment.

Not all venture capital firms are equal, however. As was demonstrated in the dot-com era, a herdlike mentality can often be found among venture capital firms. At the present time, only a handful of firms have acquired the expertise to adequately perform the due diligence in the field of cleantech.

In addition to the financial resources they bring to the table, venture capital firms are important for two additional reasons. First, they often come to the table with fat Rolodexes and can help their portfolio companies find the appropriate executive management team. For instance, in early 2007, Vinod Khosla's firm was able to help convince a veteran ethanol CEO to leave his established company to help grow a new cellulosic ethanol company.

Secondly, the good venture capital firms have existing relationships with major corporations and can use those relationships to play the roles of matchmaker.

The downside is that for assuming so much risk, venture capital firms often demand a sizable share of the company's equity. This is a dilemma for both the company founders and individual investors. Obviously, venture capital firms deserve to be rewarded for the risk they assume; the question is how much. There is no simple, easy rule to follow. The more money and the earlier the firm invests, as well as the amount of scientific and professional assistance it brings to the table, all need to be considered.

In the final analysis, venture capital is usually a positive thing. Most start-ups fail—even those that venture capitalists invest in. Venture capital firms help fund the development of the idea, professionalize the management, and assist the company in getting its product to the right market in a timeframe that allows the company the best chance of succeeding.

Buyer Beware

The harsh reality of the marketplace is that most high-technology companies fail. Cleantech is not going to be any different, and many of the companies profiled in this book will fail for the same reasons most companies do: poor management, inferior technology, and undercapitalization. By doing due diligence, however, the individual investor can reduce his or her risk. (Let me repeat that last point: risk can be reduced but it cannot be *eliminated!*)

Doing due diligence is not an easy task but here are the ten most important questions you should ask and have answered before investing in any company:

1. Is the company's management team experienced?
2. Does the company's product meet a real-world need?
3. Is the product ready for the marketplace and can it be produced consistently and reliability?
4. Does the company have strategic partners?
5. Does the company's founder have a strong scientific and technical background?
6. Is the company's board of scientific advisors actively engaged in the company?
7. Is the company's intellectual property patented or has it secured the necessary licensing agreements on favorable terms (e.g., exclusivity, duration)?
8. Do the company's founders have their own money invested in the company—and that of their family and friends?
9. Has the company received any government grants to help fund its research and development?
10. Has the company received venture capital from a firm with established expertise in the area of clean technology?

The stock market rewards a greater return on an investment to those investors who see things—and possibilities—that others don't. This creates a powerful incentive to conduct due diligence. As Louis Pasteur once said, "Fortune favors the prepared mind."

"In a carbon-constrained environment, it is something that could be very profitable for Exxon in the long run."

—Greg Singleton, a senior energy analyst, speaking on Exxon's decision to invest in biofuels.

Chapter Three

The Big Dogs—The *Fortune* 500 Companies

The Times They Are a Changing

In many ways, *Fortune* 500 companies might seem to be the antithesis of cleantech because of their involvement in producing and profiting from traditional energy sources or because they are such large consumers of fossil fuels themselves. In spite of these realities, a handful of large companies do warrant consideration as "green" investments (perhaps you might want to think of them as "light green" investments) because, as Bob Dylan once wrote, "The times they are a changin'."

Nowhere was this more evident than in the recent actions of a *Fortune* 500 company that is not profiled in this section: Exxon. In July 2009, the company stunned cleantech observers by announcing it was making a $600 million investment in biofuel pioneer, Synthetic Genomics. To appreciate the significance of this milestone it helps to understand that Exxon CEO Rex Tillerson once dismissed biofuels by saying that he intended to be driven to his funeral by a hearse fueled with gas or diesel. Mr. Tillerson, of course, will still die someday, but the chances are growing that his hearse may be powered by biodiesel or possibly even some other genetically produced biofuel.

Exxon, though, is a Johnnie-come-lately to the green energy sector. In 2009, General Electric began the year by airing a high-profile television commercial during the Super Bowl that touted its new smart grid initiative. Meanwhile, Google has unveiled a series of high-profile investments in innovative wind power and geothermal start-ups; IBM has created a new "Strategic Carbon Management" program to help companies become more energy efficient; PG&E has recently contracted with a private solar provider to purchase 1,300 MW of solar energy; and Siemens has begun construction of a 500 MW wind turbine manufacturing plant in China.

In many ways the push into cleantech could be said to have started in 2000 when British Petroleum changed its name to BP and kicked off a large public relations campaign claiming that "BP" stood for *Beyond Petroleum*. The campaign was designed to signal that the company was serious about developing alternatives to oil and gasoline.

Many opponents have accused BP and others of "green washing"—or hiding behind a slick advertising campaign designed to make them look environmentally conscious while going about business as usual. There is, of course, some truth to this accusation because BP still makes a preponderance of its money from oil, but what most people don't appreciate is that the change in philosophy was driven in large measure by the realization that by cutting its own carbon dioxide emissions to 1990 levels, the company saved more than $650 million. In short, BP awoke to the realization that there was money to be made by being green. GE is now following suit and is using its own technology to reduce its internal energy consumption by 30 percent by 2012.

These companies are still criticized in some circles for "green washing," but BP has matched its rhetoric by investing $500 million in the "Energy Innovation Center" at the University of California at Berkeley, which is seeking to develop new biofuels for the future, and General Electric is also aggressively increasing its commitment to renewable energy research and development from $700 million to $1.5 billion in 2010.

Step by step, it is clear that the business community has awoken to the new environmental ethic. The biggest signal of this change occurred when Alcoa, Duke Energy, PG&E, and nine other energy companies—all old stalwarts of the existing energy establishment—formed the Climate Action Partnership and announced for the first time that they were willing to entertain some regulation on the control on carbon dioxide emissions. Such a proclamation would have been virtually unthinkable even a few years ago.

While it is entirely reasonable to believe that many of these companies are getting involved in renewable energy due to the public's growing concern over climate change or because they fear the inevitability of restrictive government regulations (and would prefer to have a seat at the table when that legislation is being drafted), it is now clear that they are also doing it because they realize there is money to be made from being more environmentally responsible.

In the profiles that follow, readers will learn that BP is getting very serious about developing new methods to create clean, sustainable biofuels; GE intends to invest not only in smart grid technologies but is also growing its clean coal and nuclear power businesses; and IBM is serious about becoming a leader in helping businesses manage their energy consumption more efficiently. Even big oil companies are taking some bold impressive actions in the cleantech space as Exxon's investment in Synthetic Genomics suggests.

For potential investors in any cleantech, all of this is important because these corporations have the deep pockets to engage in the research and development necessary to create the green technologies of the future. Furthermore, even if these companies' overall commitment to the cleantech cause might not be of the same quality (or sincerity) as other smaller cleantech startups, they have the size, marketing, manufacturing, distribution, and staff to sell their technology and products in the commercial marketplace in a manner that will allow them to be extremely competitive.

For this reason alone, investors interested in green investing need to be aware of what the following *Fortune* 500 companies are doing because, by virtue of size alone, they will be formidable players in almost every cleantech sector.

BP	COMPANY	BP plc
	SYMBOL	BP
	TRADING MARKET	NYSE
	ADDRESS	1 St. James' Square, London, SW1Y 4PD, United Kingdom
	PHONE	44-0-20-7496-4000
	CEO	Anthony B. Hayward
	WEB	*www.bp.com*

DESCRIPTION   Formerly known as British Petroleum, BP is the world's second-largest oil and gas company in the world and operates three different segments: Exploration and Production; Refining and Marketing; and Gas, Power, and Renewables. In 2005, the company formed "BP Alternative Energy" and consolidated all of its low-carbon activities (solar, biofuels, and wind power) into its power sector. At the present time, alternative energy represents seven percent ($647 million) of the company's total business.

REASONS TO BE BULLISH

➤ BP Solar is one of the largest and most profitable solar companies in the world. It currently controls 10 percent of the global solar market—a market expected to grow 30 percent annually through 2014.The company has an agreement with REC Corporation to supply it with silicon through 2012.

➤ BP has a strong research and development team and is pursuing a joint development program with the California Institute of Technology to develop more efficient solar cells. It has another program with MIT to research clean coal technology. In 2009, the company announced plans to invest $73 million in a cleantech commercialization center in Shanghai, China.

➤ In 2007, BP committed $500 million to the University of California and the University of Illinois to create an institute dedicated to exploring such issues as carbon dioxide sequestration and the creation of new biofuels from both microbes and crops. BP also made a sizeable investment in Synthetic Genomics—a leader in creating "designer bacteria"—to pursue this goal.

continued

BP plc continued

➤ In 2008, BP invested $90 million in Verenium to jointly develop and sell technologies related to the production of ethanol.

➤ In 2007, the company acquired Orion Energy's 1,300 MW of wind power and announced the creation of five new wind development projects in the United States with a total capacity of 550 MW of power. In 2008, the company teamed up with NRG Energy to build a 150 MW wind farm in Texas.

➤ In 2006, BP announced a joint project with DuPont to develop new technology for making butanol. If successful, butanol is likely to have a significant advantage over ethanol in the commercial marketplace. Not only does it have a higher net energy density, it can also be shipped in existing pipelines. To further this goal, the company recently invested $90 million in a partnership with Verenium to pursue technologies that will create cellulosic ethanol from nonfood sources. It also took a 50 percent stake in a 115-million-gallon-per-year sugarcane ethanol refinery in Brazil. (In total, the company expects to invest $1 billion in the facility, which is expected to be fully operational by 2010.)

➤ BP has always provided shareholders a healthy annual dividend. In 2008, it was 6.9 percent.

REASONS TO BE BEARISH

➤ In the second half of 2008, oil prices dropped by 70 percent, and in the fourth quarter of 2008 the company reported a loss of $3.3 billion—its first in seven years.

➤ Due to the global financial credit crunch, it may be increasingly difficult for BP to expand its oil and gas production.

➤ Much of the company's oil operations are located in regions of the world, such as Angola and Russia, that are not politically stable. Global tensions in any area could hurt BP earnings.

➤ Although a small part of its overall business, each renewable energy segment faces stiff competition.

➤ In mid-2008, the company decided against spinning off its renewable group but there is always the possibility that management might reconsider that decision.

WHAT TO WATCH FOR   BP is pursuing a number of cleantech developments that bear watching. Foremost among these are its solar improvement program with Caltech; its plans to develop a capacity of 2,000 MW of wind power in the United States; its biobutanol project with DuPont; its relationship with Verenium; and its plans to create the world's first commercial project designed to turn natural gas into hydrogen by stripping off carbon dioxide and pumping it into depleted oil reservoirs.

CONCLUSION   Bullish. As one of the five major oil and gas companies, BP is by no stretch a pure cleantech investment play. Nevertheless, the total size of its alternative energy business (although it makes up only 7 percent of its earnings) is still enough to make BP one of the largest renewable energy companies in the world. Over the coming years, it is likely that this aspect of its business will grow to comprise an ever larger portion of BP's overall business. For investors looking for a larger company with the resources and capital necessary to exploit the growing interest in cleantech, BP represents a solid investment. Even compared with its peers in the oil and gas business, it sports a reasonable (and historically low) price-to-earnings ratio of nine.

CVX	COMPANY	Chevron Corp.
	SYMBOL	CVX
	TRADING MARKET	NYSE
	ADDRESS	6001 Bollinger Canyon Road, San Ramon, CA 94583
	PHONE	925-842-1000
	CEO	Dave O'Reilly
	WEB	*www.chevron.com*

DESCRIPTION   Chevron is the second-largest U.S. oil company and operates across all segments of the oil and gas industry—exploration, production, refining, and marketing—and in 195 countries around the world. It also has modest stakes in a variety of renewable energies, including geothermal, biofuels, solar cells, and hydrogen/fuel-cell-related technologies.

REASONS TO BE BULLISH

➤ The company's 2009 Corporate Responsibility Report reports investments of $2.5 billion in a variety of alternative and renewable energies, including such unconventional projects as a plan to produce transportation fuel from algae.

➤ Chevron is the largest producer of geothermal energy in the world with facilities in Indonesia and the Philippines and has an installed capacity of almost 1,300 MW.

➤ In 2008, the company signed a letter of intent with Weyerhaeuser to develop renewable transportation fuels from nonfood sources.

➤ The company's subsidiary, Chevron Energy Solutions, was instrumental in helping install California's first megawatt-class hydrogen fuel cell cogeneration plant and, in late 2008, was awarded a master contract by the U.S. Department of Energy to work with federal agencies to increase the use of renewable energy at agency facilities.

➤ Chevron has invested in Konarka—one of the more promising solar-related start-ups—and, together with Energy Conversion Devices, owns a 50 percent in Cobasys, a leader in developing high-powered nickel metal hydride batteries.

➤ The company has invested over $50 million in a variety of biofuel research initiatives (including cellulosic ethanol) at some of America's leading universities.

➤ In 2007, Chevron opened a 20 million gallon biodiesel facility in Texas. The company is operating it with expectation that the facility could be producing 110 million gallons annually by 2010.

REASONS TO BE BEARISH

➤ Having fallen from over $140 per barrel to less than $60 from late 2008 to mid-2009, the drop in oil prices will reduce profits and hinder the company's expansion plans.

➤ Chevron faces strong competition from ExxonMobil, BP, ConocoPhillips, and Royal Dutch Shell.

➤ Like all other oil companies, it is subject to the inherent risks and volatility of the oil and gas market, including fluctuating oil prices, geopolitical risks, weather-related issues, and spills.

➤ Because Chevron is located in California, it could also be more prone to environmental regulations and mandates than other oil companies because of that state's active involvement in passing environmental legislation.

WHAT TO WATCH FOR   All of Chevron's renewable energy demonstration projects bear watching; however, investors should assign the most prominence (and watch for news related) to its biofuels initiative as well as the expansion of its geothermal capacity.

CONCLUSION   Neutral. Although a solid company, by no stretch of the imagination can Chevron be considered a pure cleantech investment due to its near total reliance on oil and gas. However, the company's position as the world's largest producer of geothermal energy as well as its involvement in so many cleantech projects suggests its interest in renewable energy is more than a public-relations move. Investors who are comfortable investing in a traditional energy company, which has the potential to grow into a larger, more formidable cleantech investment over the next ten years, are encouraged to consider its stock. With a price-to-earnings ratio of seven, there are few other companies with this level of involvement in the renewable energy field so affordable.

SYM	COMPANY	Ei DuPont de Nemours & Co.
	SYMBOL	DD
	TRADING MARKET	NYSE
	ADDRESS	1007 Market Street, Wilmington, DE 19898
	PHONE	302-774-1000
	CEO	Ellen J. Kullman
	WEB	*www.dupont.com*

DESCRIPTION   DuPont is a science and technology company operating in six distinct areas: agriculture, industrial biotechnology, chemistry, biology, materials science, and manufacturing. By virtue of this diversity, the company is involved in a number of cleantech sectors, including biofuels, solar energy, fuel cell technology, and wave power.

REASONS TO BE BULLISH

➤ In spite of decreasing sales, the company still offers a healthy dividend, which, at the 2009 price, is roughly 7 percent.

➤ From 2007 to 2009 sales of photovoltaics have tripled from $100 million to $300 million, and the company expects that figure to again triple to over $1 billion by 2013.

➤ In 2008, DuPont established a $140 million 50–50 joint venture with Danisco Cellulsoic Ethanol to begin producing cellulosic ethanol. The plant, once operational, is expected to produce between 20–30 million gallons annually.

➤ The company is a minority stakeholder in Smart FuelCells, which is supplying portable fuel cells to the U.S. Army.

➤ DuPont is exploring passive protection material technology for wave power systems.

REASONS TO BE BEARISH

➤ Sales decreased sharply beginning in late 2008, and a recovery in the near term looks unlikely as global demand across its large sectors continues to soften.

➤ The overexpansion of solar cells in the global solar market will make DuPont's growth projections difficult to meet.

WHAT TO WATCH FOR   The key to DuPont becoming a legitimate player in the cleantech sector will rest on its continued growth in the solar and cellulosic ethanol fields. Investors are advised to monitor its success in meeting its $1 billion solar threshold by 2013 and its success in getting its new cellulosic ethanol plant operational.

CONCLUSION   Bearish. Every cleantech venture DuPont is working on has merit, but the small scale and the distant timeframe for establishing each venture make it highly unlikely that cleantech will do anything but remain a niche sector within this otherwise massive and slow-growing conglomerate. Investors looking for a conservative, diversified play are advised to consider GE or Siemens before DuPont.

GE	COMPANY	General Electric
	SYMBOL	GE
	TRADING MARKET	NYSE
	ADDRESS	3135 Easton Turnpike, Fairfield, CT 06828
	PHONE	203-373-2211
	CEO	Jeffrey Immelt
	WEB	*www.ge.com*

DESCRIPTION   General Electric is one of the world's largest companies with a market capitalization of $130 billion. It has six separate operating segments and manufactures everything from jet engines, gas turbines, and medical imaging systems to home appliances and water filtration products. A sizeable portion of the company's revenue comes from its financial services division, and it also owns the NBC/Universal broadcasting system. It is, however, the company's infrastructure segment that makes GE a true cleantech company. In 2005, CEO Jeff Immelt launched the company's "ecoimagination" initiative and announced that it would be increasing its investments in cleantech to over $2 billion by 2010. The bulk of this money is expected to be invested in coal gasification, wind, solar, and fuel cell technologies.

REASONS TO BE BULLISH
➤ The company is diversified across a wide array of "cleantech" sectors, including wind power, solar, fuel cell, and biomass. At this time, it is the leading manufacturer of wind turbines in the United States and received a massive order for 700 wind turbines from Mesa Power in mid-2008. In early 2009, it became the majority stakeholder in PrimeStar Solar, a thin-film solar company.
➤ In light of the 2009 U.S. Economic Stimulus bill and China's $558 billion infrastructure stimulus investment plan, many aspects of GE's business, including renewable energy, are well positioned to benefit from this government largesse.
➤ GE's Energy Financials Services Division raised its 2010 renewable-energy-investing target by 50 percent to $6 billion.

➤ GE is partnering with Google on a number of smart-grid projects, and it was recently selected by Commonwealth Edison to head its smart-grid initiative.

➤ In 2009, the company announced plans to supply 900 large wind turbine gearboxes to China-based A-Power Energy Generating Systems. Over the next decade, the wind market in China could grow thirtyfold.

➤ From a different perspective, China now accounts for only 3 percent of the company's $173 billion in global sales, suggesting the opportunity for extraordinary growth. In late 2008, GE opened five new offices in the country to exploit this opportunity.

➤ GE is also investing in other regions of the world and in 2008 announced the creation of a $50 million cleantech fund in Abu Dhabi, which is home to the innovative Masdar project.

➤ GE has a strong research and development lab, and in addition to its $1.5 billion commitment to fund cleantech-related advances, the company's Global Research Lab is also investing heavily in nanotechnology—an area that could lead to additional breakthroughs in terms of lighter, stronger, and more flexible wind turbines; more efficient photovoltaics, as well as advances in the economical production of hydrogen.

➤ To this end, the company has demonstrated the world's first roll-to-roll manufactured organic light-emitting diodes (OLED) and intends to introduce a product in 2010.

REASONS TO BE BEARISH

➤ GE now derives over half of its earning from its financial subsidiaries. What happens in this sector—especially with regard to continued unease in the banking and financial sectors—will easily overshadow progress in the cleantech arena. To this end, GE Capital has $660 billion in assets, but only $53 billion in equity—making it, for all practical purposes, insolvent.

➤ In early 2009, GE slashed its dividend by 68 percent.

➤ If solar technology emerges as the "first among equals" in alternative energy, GE, as it is presently configured, is not as well positioned to compete as it is in the fields of wind power, fuel cells, nuclear, and clean coal.

continued

General Electric continued

WHAT TO WATCH FOR   In early 2009, GE announced plans to reduce its energy consumption by 11 percent and water usage by 20 percent. While important from an internal perspective, if GE can succeed in accomplishing these goals it will send a powerful signal to the market that the company's technology can also help other companies save a similar amount of money. Investors will also want to pay close attention to legislation limiting carbon emissions. If such legislation becomes law in late 2009 or 2010, GE is well positioned to benefit. Other things to watch for include continued growth in the China market and signs that its OLED lighting products are reaching the commercial marketplace in 2010.

CONCLUSION   Bullish. Since early 2008, GE has lost over 75 percent of its value. On the plus side, the company P/E ratio is now below ten, which is reasonable by historical standards. GE remains well-managed and diversified, and its scientific and research staff is among the best in the world. GE's infrastructure segment is well positioned to benefit from sizeable global investments in renewable energy and infrastructure over the coming years. The company is a safe, conservative way to make an investment in the cleantech field.

GOOG	COMPANY	Google, Inc.
	SYMBOL	GOOG
	TRADING MARKET	Nasdaq
	ADDRESS	1600 Amphitheatre Parkway, Mountain View, CA 94043
	PHONE	650-253-0000
	CEO	Eric E. Schmidt
	WEB	*www.google.com*

DESCRIPTION   Google is one of the world's leading technology companies and maintains an index of websites and online content for users and advertisers. Since 2007 the company has made a number of forays into the cleantech space, including investments, policy initiatives, and partnerships, which may make the company a leading player in the green energy field in the years ahead.

REASONS TO BE BULLISH

➤ In late 2007, Google announced its intention to invest hundreds of millions of dollars in renewable energy over the next few years. To this end, it established a research and development initiative called Renewable Energy Cheaper than Coal (or RE<C) with the stated goal of making renewable energy from solar, wind, and geothermal cost-competitive with coal. It now also has a venture capital arm dedicated specifically to financing cleantech deals.

➤ As part of the initiative, Google has already made sizeable investments in solar thermal start-ups, eSolar and Brightsource Energy; high-altitude wind company, Makani Power; and geothermal start-up, AltaRock Energy.

➤ Through its not-for-profit arm, Google.org, the company launched its RechargeIT initiative, which is offering $10 million for the creation and development of hybrid plug-in vehicles. To date, it has invested in ActaCell, a battery developer, and Aptera Motors, an innovative electric car maker.

➤ In the last quarter of 2008, Google was the second-largest cleantech venture investor in the country. While still smaller in terms of total investments, the company's well-established brand could help its start-ups.

continued

Google Inc. continued

➤ The company is also partnering with GE on the development of energy-management systems that can reduce the use of energy through smart meters and information management technology. In early 2009, it launched PowerMeter, a prototype software for helping homeowners monitor and better control their energy usage.

REASONS TO BE BEARISH

➤ Google is primarily an information management company. A drive into clean technology could be seen as an area largely outside of its realm of expertise.
➤ The company is also pursuing initiatives in other areas, such as health care, that could come to take up more of its time and energy.

WHAT TO WATCH FOR   The company's investment in eSolar, Brightsource, Makani, and AltaRock Energy should all be monitored as well as these companies' abilities to deliver energy that is cost-competitive with coal. If Google can achieve this goal within five years it will widely be hailed as an impressive victory and should reflect itself in the company's stock price. More immediately, Google has a great opportunity to build off of its strengths in the information management area and help consumers use that information to control energy costs. Investors are advised to monitor the rollout of its PowerMeter technology. The sooner this technology is available, the better.

CONCLUSION   Bullish. Google is an impressive company and it should not be underestimated. However, it is not prudent to consider the company a pure-play cleantech investment. Only investors looking for a method to diversify their portfolio and gain a foothold in the information management/energy-demand side of cleantech are encouraged to invest in the company.

IBM	COMPANY	IBM
	SYMBOL	IBM
	TRADING MARKET	NYSE
	ADDRESS	1133 Westchester Avenue, White Plains, NY 10604
	PHONE	800-IBM-4YOU
	CEO	Sam Palmisano
	WEB	*www.ibm.com*

DESCRIPTION   IBM is the biggest computer equipment vendor and information technology provider in the world and has a rich history of creating, developing, and manufacturing advanced information technologies, including highly energy-efficient computer chips. In 2007, the company unveiled its "Big Green Innovations" program, and in 2009 it followed that up with the creation of a new "Strategic Carbon Management" consulting service.

REASONS TO BE BULLISH

➤ With its state-of-the-art research laboratories; a $7 billion annual research and development budget; and a team of world-class scientists, IBM is well positioned to develop a variety of cutting-edge clean technologies, such as new energy-efficient materials and advances in photovoltaics. In June of 2008, the company announced it was teaming up with Tokyo Ohka Kogyo to work on thin-film solar technology.

➤ The company's new "Green Sigma" consulting practice aims to help businesses reduce energy and water usage. As a proof of concept, IBM was able to cut its own energy bill by $310 million.

➤ In 2009, IBM authorized the company's financing arm to provide up to $2 billion in loans and credits to jumpstart promising smart-grid projects. It is partnering with CenterPoint Energy on a $640 million smart-meter project in the Houston area. It also plans to work with American Electric Power on three model city projects—each of which will cover 100,000 or more customers.

continued

IBM continued

➤ IBM has a rich history of using technology to expand into existing markets and create new ones. For instance, as a leader in sensor, RFID, and software technology, IBM can help businesses save a great deal of money by minimizing energy costs.

➤ As a leader in the field of supercomputing, IBM can harness the power of these machines for its own competitive advantage. For example, supercomputers can be used to model new energy-savings materials or predict better ways for companies to reduce energy costs. The computers can also be used to facilitate the creation of new biofuels.

➤ As leader in the development of carbon nanotubes and nanotechnology research, IBM is well positioned for future growth to the extent that these super-strong, super-light, and extremely conductive materials become an important component of future computer chips and next-generation thin-film solar cells. In 2008, IBM established a new nanotech center in Saudi Arabia to focus specifically on solar energy and desalination.

➤ As a strong consulting company, IBM's consultants are able to stay abreast of the latest advances in cleantech and thus help other businesses take advantage of these advances.

REASONS TO BE BEARISH

➤ As one of the world's largest companies, it is unlikely IBM will experience rapid growth.

➤ Due to its size, questions linger as to whether it will be nimble enough to react and take advantage of new opportunities in the cleantech space as they emerge.

➤ In the solar area, IBM can expect to face stiff competition from other large entrants into the field such as Intel. In the smart-grid area it will face competition from GE, EnerNoc, Comverge, and others.

WHAT TO WATCH FOR   To the extent that businesses and residences begin to intelligently employ networks of sensors to monitor and manage energy usage, IBM, as a leader in many of the enabling smart-grid technologies, should be able to profit from this transition. Investors should keep an eye on the progress of the Malta, CenterPoint Energy, and American Electric Power smart-metering projects. If successful, the worldwide market for similar opportunities is massive.

CONCLUSION   Bullish. Although IBM is not a cleantech company *per se*, by virtue of its size and technological strength, it will be a key player in this space. The company is poised to benefit from the continued and growing interest in renewable energy because it has its fingers in almost every aspect of the environmental pie. This is especially true in light of how much money both the U.S. and Chinese governments intend to invest in smart-grid technology as a result of their respective economic stimulus plans.

PCG	COMPANY	PG&E Corporation
	SYMBOL	PCG
	TRADING MARKET	NYSE
	ADDRESS	One Market Spear Tower, Suite 2400, San Francisco, CA 94105
	PHONE	415-267-7070
	CEO	Peter A. Darbee
	WEB	*www.pgecorp.com*

DESCRIPTION   PG&E Corporation is the owner of the Pacific Gas & Electric Company, a regulated utility servicing 17 million people in Northern and Central California. The utility has businesses in electric and natural gas distribution, electricity generation, procurement and transmission, as well as natural gas procurement, transportation, and storage. The reason it is listed as a cleantech company is because 20 percent of its electricity is expected to be produced from renewable energy sources by 2010.

REASONS TO BE BULLISH

➤ Among all utilities, PG&E produces the most electricity from renewable resources.

➤ In addition to deriving 14 percent from renewable resources, the company generated an additional 46 percent of its electricity from nuclear power and hydroelectric power. This means nearly 60 percent of all of its energy is free from carbon dioxide emissions. In the event the state of California or the federal government imposes limits on carbon dioxide emissions, PG&E could be a bigger winner.

➤ The company sports a reasonable price-to-earnings ratio, projects healthy growth through 2011, and resides in a well-regulated environment. This makes PG&E a relatively low-risk investment.

➤ The company is aggressively pursuing a variety of renewable energy projects, including projects in the following areas: geothermal, wind, solar, fuel cell, biomass, and wave power. More important, in 2009, PG&E signed a number of power purchase agreements with leading solar, solar thermal, and wind companies, which should ensure that it is well positioned to meet its 20 percent renewable energy goal by 2010. The largest is a 1.3 GW agreement with Brightsource Energy.

➤ PG&E is in the midst of the nation's largest smart meter program and is investing $2.3 billion to install 10.3 million meters by 2011. (To date, 1.4 million have been installed.)

REASONS TO BE BEARISH

➤ The company has experienced healthy growth since 2005 and it currently trades at a premium to its industry peers, suggesting it may not appreciate in price as quickly.

➤ PG&E has yet to sign any agreements with thin-film solar companies.

WHAT TO WATCH FOR   The company's initiative in the smart meter area could pay significant dividends by allowing the company (and its customers) to better manage energy usage. In turn, this could help the company save money by avoiding investment in additional capacity. In the midterm, investors are encouraged to monitor its progress in meeting California's stringent 20 percent renewable energy standard. By all accounts, the company is well positioned to meet the goals, but there could be negative regulatory consequences if it fails. Longer term, PG&E's biomass and wave power projects bear watching, as does a pilot project it is undertaking to review the feasibility of storing excess electricity in hybrid plug-in vehicles. (The idea is to recharge the batteries of the automobiles in the evening—when the price of electricity is low—and then during the peak hours when electricity is more expensive use it to power homes and businesses.)

CONCLUSION   Bullish. It is not fair to call PG&E a pure cleantech investment, but for investors looking for a safe, low-risk investment in a company that is aggressively pursuing renewable energy, it makes for a solid investment.

SI	COMPANY	Siemens AG
	SYMBOL	SI
	TRADING MARKET	NYSE
	ADDRESS	Wittelsbacherplatz 2 Munich, 80333 Germany
	PHONE	49-89-636-32474
	CEO	Peter Loescher
	WEB	*www.siemens.com*

DESCRIPTION   Like its American counterpart General Electric, Siemens AG is a massive, well-diversified conglomerate involved in everything from trains to lighting. It has positions in communications, industrial automation, power generation, medical diagnostics, rail transportation systems, automotive electronics, and lighting. It is considered a cleantech company because its positions in power generation, power transmission and distribution, and building technologies and lighting represent over one-quarter of the company's value.

REASONS TO BE BULLISH

➤ As a multinational corporation with a strong presence in the European Union, the Middle East, Asia, and the United States, Siemens is well positioned to benefit from the global increase in the demand for clean energy. For the year 2008, revenues from cleantech ventures increased to $40 billion—an increase of $13 billion from 2007. The company expects the figure to increase 10 percent through 2011.

➤ Additionally, Siemens is well diversified across various cleantech sectors with positions in wind power, instrumentation and controls, gas turbine power plants, fuel cell technology, wave power, and ethanol plant construction. In the past year, it has opened a wind research and development facility in the United States; broke ground on a large wind turbine production facility in China; announced plans to work with StatoilHydro on the world's first full-scale floating wind turbine; invested in a large waste heat recovery facility in India; and has broken ground on a 1,500 MW wind turbine manufacturing plant in China.

➤ In late 2008, it won a major contract from E.ON to supply the company with 500 wind turbines. E.ON has major expansion plans and if Siemens can remain as the preferred supplier it represents a significant growth market.

➤ Siemens expects to invest $1.5 billion annually in R&D and has also its venture capital arms scouring the commercial market for promising cleantech ventures.

➤ In the past year, Siemens has won major multibillion dollar contract from both the U.S. and Chinese governments to supply water-saving technologies.

➤ Over the past few years, the company has made great strides in improving the efficiency of lighting. Its work in the area of light-emitting diodes could extend the environmental benefits beyond what even the newer compact fluorescent lamps are achieving.

➤ The company owns WaveGen and thus has a position in the emerging field of wave power.

REASONS TO BE BEARISH

➤ While the wind market is poised for extraordinary growth, Siemens will face considerable competition from GE, Vestas, and other wind turbine producers. The same is true in the field of water desalination.

➤ Although the company has energy-saving technologies, it does not appear to have placed as big of an emphasis on this area as other competitors. This could hurt the company in the long run as there is a great opportunity in this area.

➤ It is currently trading at a premium compared with GE.

WHAT TO WATCH FOR   As a company that it not limited to cleantech, it is important for investors to understand that its stock will be driven as much by its progress in areas unrelated to cleantech, such as communications and medical diagnostics. Nevertheless, the company's forays into desalination and the creation of large offshore wind farms (especially in China) offer excellent prospects for growth. Investors should monitor the company for signs of progress in these areas.

CONCLUSION   Bullish. Siemens may not be a pure-play cleantech investment, but for investors looking for a safe and conservative way to play the cleantech field, it's a wise investment choice. It trades at a reasonable valuation (a P/E ratio of seven) and has a sizeable presence in the wind and clean water industries.

Conclusion

As the preceding pages documented, all of the *Fortune* 500 companies profiled are engaged in activities that transcend cleantech. In fact, for most of the companies, renewable energy represents a modest percentage of their overall business. Nevertheless, the sheer size of these companies means that even a small percentage can translate into a multibillion dollar business enterprise. This implies that in terms of revenues and profits, these *Fortune* 500 companies are—in dollar terms alone—among the largest cleantech companies in the world.

Undoubtedly, some investors will be inclined not to invest in these companies for any number of reasons, including their opposition to the company's involvement in more traditional (and polluting) energy sources. Others perhaps will shy away from investments because they do not believe that these companies, owing to their large size, will be able to offer the same type of returns as some of the smaller and midsized companies. (On the flip side, though, it is also fair to note that these large companies are also likely to be less volatile than their smaller counterparts.)

The decision to invest or not in these companies is, of course, a personal one; if you choose to ignore this option and instead focus on pure-play biofuel, wind, solar, or smart-grid companies, you must still pay attention to these large companies because they will remain formidable competitors to many of the smaller cleantech companies and could have a considerable impact on those pure-play cleantech investments.

"The bottom line is that it is simply premature to rule out any biofuel option."

—John DeCicco, U.S. Environmental Defense Fund

Chapter Four

Biofuels: A Long, Slow Bridge to Nowhere?

In the introduction to this chapter in the first edition of this book I wrote: "The laws of supply and demand may end up working against ethanol producers in two ways. First, the higher price of corn will depress profit margins, and then the possibility that ethanol supply will exceed demand could depress the price at the pump." These two factors, alone, made me decidedly bearish on the entire ethanol sector.

As events unfolded, the situation was even worse than imagined. Not only did corn prices soar and eat into ethanol producers' margins, many producers were seduced by the high price of oil, which peaked at $145 a barrel in the summer of 2008, into ramping up production. The number of ethanol plants exploded from fifty-seven in 2007 to 160 the following year. By the time these plants began producing ethanol, though, the price of oil had plummeted to below $40—making the biofuel uncompetitive with oil and leaving ethanol producers with a glut of expensive ethanol. On top of these woes, the global recession severely constricted the amount of working capital available to producers.

The net effect of this perfect storm was that in the first quarter of 2009 twenty-four ethanol plants—representing a staggering 15 percent of the market—closed. Moreover, three ethanol companies (VeraSun, Pacific Ethanol, and E3 Biofuels) were forced into bankruptcy, and dozens more saw the value of their stock fall by 80 percent or more.

As predicted, the industry is now undergoing a massive consolidation. Valero recently acquired seven of VeraSun's ethanol plants and a handful of the larger, better financed companies are eyeing many of the more distressed ethanol companies.

The sector should gradually return to normalcy, and things may even modestly improve as the effects of the U.S. government's $790 billion stimulus plan begins to make its way into the sector. The industry will also benefit from the Environmental Protection Agency's 2009 decision to increase, from 7.76 percent to 10.21 percent, the amount of ethanol that must be blended into a gallon of gasoline. The mandate will create a larger market for ethanol.

Alas, these two factors will not be enough to dramatically improve corn ethanol's long-term prospects. Intense competition, low margins, serious questions regarding the net environmental impact of corn-based ethanol, and growing concerns over the fuel's impact on rising food prices will all continue to cast a long shadow over the industry.

The New Kid on the Block: Cellulosic Ethanol

Ethanol prospects are not all doom and gloom, but it may be that corn-produced ethanol won't be the product leading the way. As it stands, producers today can squeeze about 420 gallons of ethanol from an acre of corn. More efficient distillation techniques, better catalysts, and even genetically enhanced corn could increase this amount to 750 gallons per acre. Even with such advances, ethanol would only replace 20 percent of the current fuel market.

One long-term solution may be the production of cellulosic ethanol. Cellulosic ethanol is chemically identical to corn ethanol, but instead of being produced from the kernel of corn, the ethanol is produced from lignocellulose, a structural material comprising much of the mass of many agricultural products, including corn stover, switchgrass, oat, wheat, and barley straw, and some wood sources.

The potential advantages of cellulosic ethanol are many. For starters, the feedstock sources are more distributed and plentiful. Whereas corn is primarily grown in the Midwest, cellulosic feedstocks can be found virtually everywhere. One company, Range Fuels, for instance, is constructing a cellulosic ethanol plant in Georgia to take advantage of an excess supply of wood. This means that the production of ethanol could take place much closer to the consumer markets where the fuel is actually being used. This will eliminate costly and unnecessary transportation costs.

An even bigger advantage of cellulosic ethanol is that because it uses non-corn-related feedstocks it does not drive up the price for corn (which is also used by many food producers in the production of their products). This concern lies at the heart of the food-versus-fuel debate.

Through a combination of other advances, it is possible farmers will also learn to produce more biomass per acre. This, in turn, has led some experts to speculate that in time the industry might be able to get as many as 2,700 gallons of ethanol per acre from various feedstocks.

Such a day appears to be a way off. Cellulosic ethanol is still not yet cost-competitive with corn ethanol. Vinod Khosla, a leading venture capitalist who has made numerous investments in the field, has publicly stated he believes cellulosic ethanol will be competitive with corn ethanol as early as 2010. Many others are less confident. A more realistic timeframe is 2012.

The investors' dilemma regarding ethanol won't end with a transition to cellulosic ethanol. A number of today's leading ethanol producers are aggressively making plans to transition to cellulosic ethanol, and scores of promising start-ups are doing the same. Range Fuels, for instance, is developing a thermo-chemical process; Iogen is seeking to create new enzymes that more efficiently extract sugars from wheat and straw and convert it into ethanol; while Mascoma is seeking microbes to aide in the ethanol conversion process. Which company's processes or technologies will win in the commercial marketplace is the subject of fierce debate, and at this time there is no clear indication of how things will shake out. But for the investor it is important to note that at this time no one is producing cellulosic ethanol in but small, demonstration-level quantities.

And the Contenders

Nor is there any real indication that ethanol—either corn-based or cellulosic—will even be the biofuel of the future. Archer Daniel Midlands and Imperium Renewables are making sizeable bets that biodiesel will be the big biofuel winner.

Another biofuel that could become price competitive with gasoline and diesel is biobutanol. The advantages of biobutanol, which is currently under development by DuPont and BP, are that it can be manufactured from cornstarch or sugar beets and its properties are more like gasoline. This means it has a higher net energy density than either ethanol or biodiesel, and it can be transported using the existing gasoline infrastructure.

Of course, other possibilities exist. One scenario is that entirely new technologies will be developed to create fuel sources in unique and innovative ways. One intriguing area, being pursued by Algenol, GreenFuel Technologies, and Sapphire Energy, is algae that might be used to consume or eat carbon dioxide and then (depending upon the genetic makeup of the algae) secrete either oil or ethanol. A second alternative is synthetic biology. Synthetic Genomics, for instance, is working to create "designer bacteria," which could create a simple, low-cost method of producing various biofuels.

As promising as cellulosic ethanol and these other biofuels may be, it is important to remember that none are currently being produced at commercial-scale levels. Furthermore, there always remains the possibility that they will: 1) never become competitive; 2) become nothing more than a niche biofuel; or 3) be rendered totally obsolete by a dramatic advance in engine design for gas-power automobiles; improved battery technology; or possibly even a breakthrough in hydrogen fuel-cell technology.

With these strong caveats in mind, here then are some biofuel companies that are still worth knowing (a few will even make good investments).

ABG	COMPANY	Abengoa Bioenergy (a subsidiary of Abengoa)
	SYMBOL	ABG
	TRADING MARKET	Various European Stock Exchanges
	ADDRESS	1400 Elbridge Payne Road, Suite 212, Chesterfield, MO 63017
	PHONE	636-728-0508
	CEO	Javier Salgado
	WEB	*www.abengoabioenergy.com*

DESCRIPTION   Abengoa Bioenergy is dedicated to the development of biofuels. Operating through different subsidiaries, the company owns and operates a variety of facilities for producing and marketing bioethanol throughout the United States and the European Union.

REASONS TO BE BULLISH

➤ At the present time, Abengoa is the largest ethanol producer in the European Union and the fifth largest in the United States. It produces over 340 million gallons of ethanol annually—200 million in the United States and 140 million in the European Union.

➤ In 2007, the company received a $76 million grant from the U.S. Department of Energy to develop a pilot plant for the production of cellulosic ethanol. More recently, it received a smaller grant from the state of Illinois to begin the construction of a regular ethanol plant in the state.

➤ In the area of corn ethanol production, Abengoa claims to have developed a technology that achieves a very high conversion rate for converting cornstarch into sugar. If true, it is the type of development that could allow Abengoa to be more profitable than other ethanol producers.

➤ The company has a cooperative agreement with Ford Motor Company to develop flexible fuel engines for Ford's line of automobiles in Spain.

➤ Abengoa Bioenergy is just one component of Abengoa. The company has a strong research and development team, and it also has cleantech-related businesses in the areas of solar, environmental services, industrial engineering, and construction and information technologies, and as such, it is a more diversified investment than a typical bioethanol company. In 2008, the company announced plans to construct a 280 MW solar thermal facility in Arizona.

➤ Abengoa is geographically diverse. It does 44 percent of its business in Spain, 28 percent in Latin America, 11 percent in the European Union, and 10 percent in the United States.

REASONS TO BE BEARISH

➤ The company's new cellulosic ethanol plant will cost $300 million to construct and will not be operational until 2010.

➤ In the cellulosic ethanol field, Abengoa will face considerable competitive pressure from companies such as Iogen, Cilion, Kergy, and BlueFire Ethanol. In the corn ethanol business, it will face competition from Archer Daniels Midland, Aventine Renewable, and Poet.

➤ The company has been the target of unwanted publicity as ethanol has been linked to higher food prices in the United States and the European Union.

➤ In the company's other businesses (e.g., solar, construction, environmental services) it will also face competition; however, the greater danger may be that it will be difficult for management to operate the company's diverse components as a cohesive unit given the unique demands of each division.

WHAT TO WATCH FOR   To prosper over the long term, Abengoa will need to grow its bioenergy and solar divisions. Currently, the two components represent less than 20 percent of its overall business. Investors should look for news that Abengoa's new cellulosic plant is operational in 2010. If it is producing at least 100 million gallons of ethanol annually by that time it will be a bullish sign.

continued

Abengoa Bioenergy continued

CONCLUSION   Neutral. The diversity of Abengoa makes it an attractive clean-tech play; however, until it bolsters both its bioethanol and solar businesses, investors should treat the stock with caution. If management decides to spin-off its industrial engineering, information technologies, or environmental services, it will be easier to evaluate the value of the company. If this occurs, any of its businesses might make solid investments.

ADM	COMPANY	Archer Daniels Midland
	SYMBOL	ADM
	TRADING MARKET	NYSE
	ADDRESS	4666 Faries Parkway, Decatur, IL 62526
	PHONE	800-637-5843
	CEO	Patricia Woertz
	WEB	*www.ad MWorld.com*

DESCRIPTION Archer Daniels Midland bills itself as "supermarket to the world," and is a global leader in the business of procuring, transporting, storing, processing, and marketing a wide range of agricultural products, including oilseeds, corn, wheat, and cocoa. Ethanol makes up about 19 percent of its business (albeit on only 7 percent of its sales). ADM is primarily a powerhouse in food and beverage additives.

REASONS TO BE BULLISH

➤ Has been consistently profitably over its long history and there is little to suggest that this trend won't continue. Global demand for both food and bioenergy is increasing and the company is well positioned to outperform its peers.

➤ By virtue of its size, ADM will be able to use its financial strength to buy distressed ethanol companies at reasonable prices and further consolidate its position as a world leader.

➤ Its diversified product portfolio and access to global markets protect it well from wild fluctuations, which are common to other smaller, ethanol producers.

➤ ADM expects to increase ethanol production by 550 million gallons with two new plants in Columbus, Nebraska, and Cedar Rapids, Iowa. They will bring the company's total production to 1.9 billion gallons.

➤ The company has the financial resources to engage in cutting-edge research and development, and with its access to vast amounts of agricultural product other than corn, it could easily become a leader in the production of cellulosic ethanol. In late 2008, the company joined forces with John Deere and Monsanto to research corn stover for use in biomass, cellulosic ethanol, and animal feed.

continued

Archer Daniels Midland continued

➤ Over the past five years, the company has spent $3.4 billion on new plants and facilities. These investments will help ensure it stays competitive.
➤ In 2006, it announced plans to begin building a 50 million gallon plant for biodiesel.

REASONS TO BE BEARISH
➤ ADM is not a pure-play cleantech investment. It is a food production company, and its stock is subject to fluctuation depending on global economic and political factors as well as weather-related issues.
➤ Ethanol production (and supply) could easily outpace demand and, if combined with lower oil prices (as happened in 2008), could have an adverse impact on ethanol's margins.
➤ As long as the food-versus-fuel debate remains relevant, ADM will come under pressure from political, environmental, and economic advocates who argue that the growing use of corn for ethanol production is driving food prices higher. In addition to bad PR, ADM could lose some political support in Washington over the issue.
➤ If Poet, Abengoa, or some other company becomes a leader in the production of cellulosic ethanol, ADM could be adversely impacted.

WHAT TO WATCH FOR   The price of ethanol is closely tied to the price of oil so you should monitor closely the price of the latter. To the extent that oil increases, ethanol will become more attractive. Also monitor government subsidies to ethanol. Although government support is unlikely to erode anytime soon, federal budget deficit-related concerns or food-versus-fuel pressures could cause Congress to revisit the large incentives it provides to the ethanol industry. Longer term, investors will want to look for news of progress on cellulosic ethanol production, especially in the area of turning corn stover in ethanol.

CONCLUSION   Bullish. Although ADM is by no means a cleantech pure-play investment, it is well positioned to benefit from both the growing expansion of the ethanol market as well as the cellulosic ethanol and biodiesel markets. At a current P/E ratio of below ten, it remains a solid and relative safe investment.

> **Biofuel Companies**

COMPANY	Amyris Biotechnologies
INVESTORS	Khosla Ventures, Kleiner Perkins Caufield & Byers, and Texas Pacific Group Ventures
ADDRESS	5980 Horton Street, Suite 450, Emeryville, CA 94608
PHONE	510-450-0761
CEO	John Melo
WEB	*www.amyrisbiotech.com*

DESCRIPTION   Amyris Biotechnologies is a development-stage biotechnology company. It seeks to employ synthetic biology to create a fermentation process using custom-designed microbes to produce high-performance biofuels that are cost-effective, renewable, and compatible with current automotive and distribution technologies. More succinctly, it is engineering microbes to eat sugar and secrete hydrocarbons. It has raised $91 million in funding as of 2009, and in July 2009 it opened its first large-scale biofuel plant in Brazil. (Also, in an area that isn't related to cleantech, the company is hoping to use synthetic biology to manufacture a microbe that can recreate a complex molecule found in only limited quantities in the natural world but which is highly effective at treating malaria—a disease that kills over 1 million people annually.)

WHY IT IS DISRUPTIVE   By isolating genes from their natural sources and inserting them into industrial microbes, Amyris is seeking to produce a series of complex molecules that have a higher net energy density than ethanol and to do so in a manner that is stable, scalable, and cost-effective. If Amyris is successful, it could lead to a significantly cheaper and more efficient method of producing ethanol and biodiesel. The company has raised $90 million from a group of Silicon Valley's best-known venture capitalists, including John Doerr and Vinod Khosla, and hired an experienced CEO, John Melo. He formerly served as president of U.S Fuel Operations for BP.

continued

WHAT TO WATCH FOR   In addition to making enzymes that are optimized for breaking down cellulose, the company will need to demonstrate its technology is scalable. To this end, signs that the partnership with Brazilian ethanol distributor Crystalsev to commercialize advanced renewable fuels from sugarcane by 2011—at a price that is competitive with oil at $60 a barrel—will be a bullish indicator. The company is also partnering with Virgin Airlines to manufacture a bio-friendly jet fuel by 2012–2013. At the present time, it is one of the few companies pursuing this lucrative niche—jet fuel currently contributes 12 percent of the carbon dioxide emissions. If it can develop such a fuel, it will be a very bullish indicator. The company has publicly stated it expects to be producing 200 million gallons a year by 2010.

CONCLUSION   Neutral. Amyris Biotechnologies' technology is elegant and could be a game changer in that it not only uses feedstocks different from other biofuels but its end product purports to produce 90 percent less greenhouse gas than traditional fuels. Nevertheless, Amyris is a private company and will not likely go public for some time. In the event that it does, I encourage you to discern how its technology is different from Synthetic Genomics' technology and then learn which company is closest to commercial production. Longer term, if the company scales up production, it will need to partner with a larger, more established energy company that can handle transportation and distribution.

ANDE	COMPANY	The Andersons Inc.
	SYMBOL	ANDE
	TRADING MARKET	Nasdaq
	ADDRESS	480 W. Dussel Drive, Maumee, OH 43537
	PHONE	419-893-5050
	CEO	Michael J. Anderson
	WEB	*www.andersonsinc.com*

DESCRIPTION   The Andersons Inc. is a diversified agricultural and transportation company with interests in the grain, ethanol, and plant nutrient sectors, as well as railcar marketing, industrial products manufacturing, and general merchandise retailing.

REASONS TO BE BULLISH

➤ The company has a strong balance sheet and has the necessary financial resources to survive the ethanol industry consolidation.

➤ Because the company's Rail Group and Plant Nutrient Group are quite sizeable, it is not as vulnerable to the cyclical fluctuations of the ethanol business as others in the industry.

➤ The Andersons has consistently provided shareholders with a regular, albeit modest, dividend.

➤ As a result of it experience managing corn, the Andersons appears better equipped than other smaller ethanol producers in handling the volatile nature of the commodity.

➤ The company is currently trading at an attractive P/E ratio.

REASONS TO BE BEARISH

➤ The company's stock fell 75 percent in 2008–2009 due to volatility in the ethanol market.

➤ The Andersons plant nutrient business has also been hammered by falling global fertilizer prices.

continued

The Andersons Inc. continued

WHAT TO WATCH FOR   The Andersons had, until 2008, grown steadily for seven years. Keep an eye open for news that the company is expanding into other biofuels such as cellulosic ethanol or biodiesel. Both would be positive signs. In the event of consolidation within the ethanol industry, look for the Andersons to acquire some of the smaller, less profitable ethanol facilities.

CONCLUSION   Bullish. The company's strong past performance, diversified nature, and plans for additional growth bode well for its future performance. At the time of this writing, its price still appears attractive when compared with historical averages. Long term, only a few ethanol companies will survive. The Andersons has a good chance of being one of the survivors and then prospering when the biofuels market returns from its nadir.

AVRNQ .PK		
	COMPANY	Aventine Renewable Energy Holdings
	SYMBOL	AVRNQ.PK
	TRADING MARKET	Over-the-counter
	ADDRESS	1300 South 2nd Street, Pekin, IL 61555-0010
	PHONE	309-347-9200
	CEO	Ronald H. Miller
	WEB	*www.aventinerei.com*

DESCRIPTION   Aventine Renewable Energy produces and markets ethanol. It has a smaller business producing various co-products, such as distillers' grain, corn gluten feed, and brewer's yeast. In 2008, the company sold almost 700 million gallons of ethanol—approximately 10 percent of the total sold in the United States.

REASONS TO BE BULLISH

➤ As a leading marketer of ethanol, it has well-established relationships with companies including Royal Dutch Shell, ConocoPhillips, Exxon/Mobil, and Texaco/Chevron.

➤ Aventine's unique distribution infrastructure allows it to better play the corn market to take advantage of ethanol pricing. (For instance, in a depressed market it can store ethanol and in a seller's market it can quickly reduce its inventory.)

➤ The company plans to expand production by 226 million gallons in 2009 and by another 339 million in 2010.

REASONS TO BE BEARISH

➤ Weaker demand and volatile corn and energy prices have hurt the company, and in the past year its stock has plummeted more than 95 percent. In May 2009, the company's stock was delisted from the New York Stock Exchange because it couldn't stay above $1 per share.

continued

Aventine Renewable Energy Holdings continued

➤ The company is expected to lose money in 2009 and is burning cash at a fast rate making it unlikely it will be able to execute its expansion plans.

➤ In 2008, the company had to suspend construction on its Aurora facility.

➤ The company has no apparent plans to move into the production of cellulosic ethanol, a position that leaves it vulnerable to fluctuating corn prices.

WHAT TO WATCH FOR   Aventine will need to continue to expand its ethanol production as well as increase the total number of gallons of ethanol it is marketing to stay abreast of competitors. As such, investors should keep a close eye on whether it meets its goal of bringing 226 million gallons online in 2009 and another 339 million in 2010. Also, if it does not improve its cash position in 2009, the company could also become an acquisition target.

CONCLUSION   Neutral. While Aventine does have some strength in the area of distribution, it needs to bolster its ethanol production in order to be a long-term player. If it can weather the current shakeout in the ethanol industry—and this is a big *if* at this time—the company could, from its current price, stand to return a premium to those investors who have a penchant for high-risk/high-reward scenarios.

BIOF	COMPANY	BioFuel Energy
	SYMBOL	BIOF
	TRADING MARKET	NASDAQ
	ADDRESS	1801 Broadway, Suite 1060, Denver, CO 80202
	PHONE	303-592-8110
	CEO	Scott Pearce
	WEB	*www.bfenergy.com*

DESCRIPTION BioFuel Energy is a development-stage ethanol company that has two 115-million-gallon-a-year production facilities in Wood River, Nebraska, and Fairmont, Minnesota. It had received regulatory approval to begin construction of three other large facilities, but due to fluctuating corn prices, falling oil prices, and a softening of the economy, those plans were shelved in 2008.

REASONS TO BE BULLISH

➤ None at this time. In 2008, the company's stock lost 95 percent of its value as the confluence of higher corn prices, lower fuel costs, and a softening global economy wreaked havoc on BioFuel's finances.

REASONS TO BE BEARISH

➤ BioFuel is a development-stage company, and its two facilities in Nebraska and Minnesota, although now operational, are losing money. It has only $2 million cash and a debt of $256 million.

➤ BioFuel Energy was backed by Cargill. In 2008, however, Cargill liquidated most of its position in the company.

➤ Nothing in the company's literature suggests it has developed or is working on any proprietary technology that will help it remain competitive with advances in cellulosic ethanol such as Poet and Iogen are pursuing.

continued

BioFuel Energy continued

WHAT TO WATCH FOR   There is an excellent chance BioFuel will either go bankrupt in 2009 or become an acquisition target for a more established ethanol player. About the only thing that could possibly save the company is a return to a scenario where the margins on ethanol skyrocket. Unfortunately, the ability for the company to either lock in corn at a low price or a return higher oil prices both appears unlikely in the near to midterm.

CONCLUSION   Bearish. BioFuel Energy's poor financial situation, coupled with the loss of Cargill's support, suggests the company is unlikely to survive the ethanol industry's inevitable consolidation.

BFRE.OB	COMPANY	BlueFire Ethanol
	SYMBOL	BFRE.OB
	TRADING MARKET	Over-the-counter (Pink Sheets)
	ADDRESS	31 Musick, Irvine, CA 92618
	PHONE	949-588-3767
	CEO	Arnold R. Klann
	WEB	*www.bluefireethanol.com*

DESCRIPTION   BlueFire Ethanol is a developmental-stage company seeking to convert cellulosic waste materials, agricultural residues, wood residues, and biomass crops into ethanol through a proprietary process. The company's long-term plan is to build biorefinery facilities on or near landfills and waste collection and separations' sites in order to reduce landfill costs and better serve urban markets.

REASONS TO BE BULLISH

➤ BlueFire was just one of six cellulosic ethanol companies to receive a large grant ($40 million) from the U.S. Department of Energy to develop a solid waste biorefinery facility in Southern California.

➤ If its technology is successful, the company will have found a unique niche by using landfill waste. In addition to helping municipalities across the country lower their operational costs, the technology could be more environmentally friendly because it is reported to capture methane gas (which is a more potent greenhouse gas than carbon dioxide).

➤ The U.S. government has mandated that 100 million gallons of cellulosic ethanol be purchased by 2010 and 250 million by 2011. There isn't that much currently on the market. If BlueFire's process is successful, it will have a ready market for its product.

➤ BlueFire's technology also has the advantage of locating in or near urban centers and helping those communities dispose of something (municipal waste) that is currently a problem. Furthermore, by virtue of being located near customers, the company alleviates transportation costs normally associated with distributing ethanol.

continued

BlueFire Ethanol continued

➤ Unlike other ethanol companies, which are overly dependent on corn, BlueFire has no such issues.

➤ In 2008, BlueFire was ranked #13 on BioFuel Digest's list of "50 Hottest Companies in Bioenergy."

REASONS TO BE BEARISH

➤ To date, BlueFire's demonstration pilot plant is small, and the technology has not been fully borne out. A full plant that was expected to be operational in early 2009 is still pending completion.

➤ As of 2009, the company is still overly reliant on government grants, and it is not clear its technology can successfully compete with either ethanol or other cellulosic-related technologies in the absence of government support. At the time of publication, the company had less than $5 million in cash on hand.

➤ There are a growing number of cellulosic ethanol competitors, including large companies such as Poet and DuPont as well as smaller ones, such as EnerTech Environmental, which is also looking at municipal waste as a feedstock.

WHAT TO WATCH FOR   The key to BlueFire's success is its ability to produce cellulosic ethanol at a competitive cost. To this end, you should watch if the company's $130 million facility is operational by the end of 2009. Beyond that, the next thing to watch is price. As a benchmark, the Department of Energy is estimating that the production of cellulosic ethanol will be $1.07/gallon by 2012.

CONCLUSION   Bearish. BlueFire Ethanol has an intriguing technology, and it is pursuing a unique niche, but getting the necessary funding to pursue its goal will be difficult. If it is successful, however, the company could do extremely well. At the current time, though, its technology is too immature and there are a number of competitors—such as Iogen, Coskata, Abengoa, and Range Fuels—operating in the same space that appear better positioned for long-term success.

COMPANY	Cilion
INVESTORS	Khosla Partners, Virgin Fuels, Yucaipa Companies and Advanced Equities
ADDRESS	31120 West Street, Goshen, CA 93227
PHONE	559-302-2500
CEO	Mark Noetzel
WEB	*www.cilion.com*

DESCRIPTION   Formed in 2006 through a partnership with Khosla Partners, Western Milling, and Praj Industries, Cilion raised a staggering $235 million with the purpose of building eight ethanol plants—each capable of producing 55 million gallons annually—by 2008. The bulk of its plants were to be located in California. As of mid-2009, only one plant was operational.

WHY IT IS DISRUPTIVE   As of late 2009, Cilion is a straight-up ethanol company seeking to produce ethanol more efficiently than its competitors. Because of its relationship with Western Milling, which has expertise in ethanol production, grain handling, logistics, and feed, it is still feasible it can achieve this goal. The fact that Cilion will primarily serve the California market implies it will not need to assume large transportation costs in order to get its product to this lucrative market.

WHAT TO WATCH FOR   The company fared poorly in meeting its goal of producing 440 million gallons annually by 2008, although this was more a function of global factors than poor execution. Going forward, interested parties should monitor if the company's current facility in Keyes, California, is purchased by another ethanol player.

continued

Cilion continued

CONCLUSION   Bearish. Cilion appears unlikely to achieve its goal of becoming one of the more formidable ethanol producers in California. The fact that the state has mandated that 20 percent of all its biofuel is to come from within the state by 2010 (in 2008 about 10 percent did) and 40 percent by 2020 suggests a small window of opportunity remains open for the company to achieve its goal; but this is unlikely given the tough market conditions and the ongoing industry consolidation.

COMPANY	Coskata, Inc.
INVESTORS	Khosla Ventures, Globespan Capital Partners, GreatPoint Ventures; Advanced Technology Ventures, Blackstone, Arancia International, and General Motors.
ADDRESS	4575 Weaver Parkway, Suite 100, Warrenville, IL 60555
PHONE	630-657-5800
CEO	William Roy
WEB	*www.coskata.com*

DESCRIPTION   Coskata is commercializing a proprietary process for converting a wide variety of input materials, including biomass and municipal waste, into ethanol.

WHY IT IS DISRUPTIVE   Because Coskata's proprietary microorganisms eliminate the need for costly enzymatic pretreatments, the biofermentation occurs at a low temperature (thus reducing operational costs). The process can use everything from cellulosic feedstocks to old tires, and the company claims it will be able to produce ethanol for $1 a gallon. The fact that General Motors selected Coskata over seventeen other ethanol companies suggests that its technology holds great potential. Moreover, in late 2008, U.S. Sugar agreed to explore building a 100-million-gallon facility with the company.

WHAT TO WATCH FOR   The first thing Coskata needs to do is get its modest 40,000 gallon-per-year facility in Madison, Pennsylvania, operational. Next, interested parties should ensure that General Motors is using Coskata's ethanol in its new line of Flex-fuel vehicles and that the company remains on pace to expand the facility to the level of 40 million gallons by 2011–2012. Of interest will be whether Coskata is making good on its promise to use a variety of different feedstocks to produce ethanol, and whether U.S. Sugar goes beyond the exploratory phase and actually builds a plant with Coskata in Florida. If it does, it will be a bullish indicator.

continued

Coskata continued

CONCLUSION   Bullish. Coskata's proprietary technology, in combination with its partnerships with General Motors and U.S. Sugar, suggests it may be able to make good on its promise to produce ethanol for $1 a gallon. The fact that company has been able to secure financing in an otherwise tight financial market as well as make inroads in China suggests its future viability will not be solely dependent on the U.S. market. The company will still face stiff competition from Mascoma and Poet, but because its process is so different than those companies it is worth considering as a potential investment should the company go public—but only if the company can verify it is producing ethanol near its stated range of $1 a gallon.

Biofuel Companies

COMPANY	EcoSynthetix
INVESTORS	Cargill Ventures, H.B. Fuller Ventures, VentureLink Diversified Balance Fund, and 401 Capital Partners
ADDRESS	3900 Collins Road, Lansing, MI 48910
PHONE	517-336-4623
CEO	John van Leeuwen
WEB	*www.ecosynthetix.com*

DESCRIPTION   EcoSynthetix is a clean technology company seeking to replace a variety of petroleum-based industrial products, such as polyvinyl acetate and polyvinyl alcohol, with nanobiomaterials.

WHY IT IS DISRUPTIVE   EcoSynthetix has developed a proprietary process for radically reducing the size of natural cornstarch. When reduced to the nanoscale, the nanoparticles have 400 times more surface area than natural starch granules. This means they require less water to produce adhesive, which, in turn, means that less energy and time is required to dry the coatings. For an average size plastic plant this could result in energy savings of $1 million or more a year. As an added benefit, because the nanoparticles are derived from corn and not petroleum, the price of EcoSynthetix plastic will be lower and more stable.

WHAT TO WATCH FOR   In 2008, the company received a $750,000 grant from the state of Michigan to help the company begin applying its bio-based coating materials to paper products. If Michigan (or other) paper suppliers begin using the technology it will be a bullish sign.

CONCLUSION   Neutral. While EcoSynthetix technology appears to deliver the stated benefits, it faces competition from companies such as NatureWorks, LLC and Metabolix. Should the company go public, investors will want to conduct a side-by-side analysis of its technology with those other companies and discern which has lined up the most corporate customers.

Biofuel Companies

COMPANY	GreenFuel Technologies Corporation
INVESTORS	Polaris Venture Partners, Access Private Equity, and Draper Fisher Jurvetson
ADDRESS	735 Concord Avenue, Cambridge, MA 02138
PHONE	617-234-0077
CEO	Simon Upfill-Brown
WEB	*www.greenfuelonline.com*

DESCRIPTION   GreenFuel Technologies is an early-development-stage company attempting to pioneer the development of an algae bioreactor technology, dubbed Emissions-to-Biofuels. The technology seeks to efficiently convert carbon dioxide from the smokestack gases of coal-fired power plants and other carbon-dioxide-producing facilities into clean, renewable biofuels.

WHY IT IS DISRUPTIVE   Algae are unicellular plants and, like all plants, they divide and grow using photosynthesis. According to GreenFuel, its proprietary process can absorb a significant percentage (up to 40 percent) of a power plant's carbon dioxide emissions every day. The technology has a surprising number of potential benefits. For starters, it can significantly reduce carbon dioxide emissions without requiring energy companies to undergo an extensive retooling or modification. As such, it has the potential to earn companies valuable emission credits and government tax subsidies, while also improving a company's image as a clean manufacturer. Furthermore, because the algae can be converted into any number of different biofuels, including ethanol, biodiesel, methane, and solid biomass, it can be used as an affordable energy source. In this way, it could either help a coal company create revenue from biofuel sales or reduce its exposure to fossil price volatility. In late 2008, the company announced plans (in partnership with Aurantia SA) to build its first commercial project, a $92 million 100-hectare algae farm in Spain by 2011.

WHAT TO WATCH FOR   GreenFuel remains a development-stage company, and it is not clear at this time whether its technology can scale to industrial capacity levels or if it can compete favorably with other carbon-dioxide-reducing technologies (such as carbon sequestration or nanoparticle catalysts). GreenFuel's first big test will be whether the project in Spain can scale according to plans. If that project is successful it will be a positive, but you'll still want to pay attention to whether the fuel it produces is cost-competitive with existing competitors. Interested parties are also encouraged to watch for news that GreenFuel's algae can be used as a jet fuel. If successful this would be a positive development, and you should then watch for news that the company is pursuing plans to build additional plants in the United States.

CONCLUSION Bearish. GreenFuel has experienced a number of setbacks in recent years, and while these appear to have been overcome, the company will likely find it difficult to find access to the capital necessary to expand. Furthermore, now that other companies (such as Sapphire Energy) are developing similar algae-converting technology, it will be more difficult for GreenFuel to distinguish itself. Provided, however, the company's technology can eat carbon dioxide as promised and then effectively and efficiently convert the algae into a biofuel by 2011, there exists the possibility GreenFuel's technology could become a valuable tool for coal companies looking to reduce their carbon footprint. Longer term, if the technology could be used to create large algae farms capable of producing large amounts of biofuel, it will provide government officials a handy way of avoiding the food-versus-fuel fight. Nevertheless, the latter two possibilities appear remote. If the company files for an IPO, investors are advised to stay away.

COMPANY	Imperium Renewables
INVESTORS	North Power, Ardsley Partners, Technology Partners, Blackrock Investment Management, Silver Point Capital, Treaty Oak Capital, Ecofin, Stack Biodiesel Investors
ADDRESS	1418 Third Avenue, Suite 300, Seattle, WA 98101
PHONE	206-254-0204
CEO	John Plaza
WEB	*www.imperiumrenewables.com*

DESCRIPTION   Founded as Seattle Biodiesel, LLC in 2003, Imperium Renewables is seeking to become a national leader in next-generation biodiesel refining and manufacturing technology. In 2008, however, the company cancelled plans for a $345 million IPO, and now its plant is not expected to be operational until 2010.

WHY IT IS DISRUPTIVE   The company's goal is to use proprietary technology, including its ultra-efficient Pressurized "Pulse Reactor," its Active Methanol Recovery System, and its adsorbent Enhanced Polish System, to deliver a gallon of biodiesel cheaper than a petroleum facility can manufacture diesel fuel (assuming $40 crude). Because Imperium's biodiesel is manufactured from vegetable oil, including soybeans, canola, and palm oil, it is 100 percent renewable. As an added benefit, it emits 78 percent less carbon dioxide. Other advantages the company has going for it include the fact that at the present time it is the only large-scale biodiesel facility in the western United States, and it has also had its biodiesel approved to ASTM standards—meaning it performs as well, if not better, than regular diesel fuel.

WHAT TO WATCH FOR   Imperium must make good on its plans to build a biodiesel facility capable of producing a large quantity of fuel. If the company can arrange the necessary financing, investors will then want to focus on whether it can produce fuel at a price competitive with regular diesel. You will also want to monitor whether Virgin Airlines and other airlines continue experimenting with its biodiesel as a potential fuel source. If this materializes, it will be a bright spot in an otherwise dismal forecast.

CONCLUSION Bearish. In addition to a tough financial market that has placed the company under great stress, Imperium has had to postpone plans for building a biodiesel plant in Hawaii, and it has experienced managerial problems. The company's goal of being the leading biodiesel producer on the West Coast of the United States is rapidly slipping away as ADM, DuPont, and a handful of other companies are aggressively moving into the biodiesel space.

COMPANY	Iogen Corporation
INVESTORS	Goldman Sachs, Royal Dutch Shell, Petro-Canada
ADDRESS	310 Hunt Club Road East, Ottawa, Canada, Ontario, Canada K1V 1C1
PHONE	613-733-9830
CEO	Brian Foody
WEB	*www.iogen.ca*

DESCRIPTION   Iogen is a biotechnology company specializing in cellulosic ethanol made from farm waste. The company has developed and patented enzymes that can extract sugars from wheat and barley straw. The company is also developing enzymes that can be used to modify and improve the processing of natural fibers in the textile, animal feed, and paper and pulp industries. The company currently has a pilot facility operational in Canada, and in late 2008 the company scrapped a high-profile plan to build a facility in Idaho, a plant that was expected to produce 18 million gallons of ethanol annually from wheat straw, barley straw, corn stover, and switchgrass.

WHY IT IS DISRUPTIVE   Iogen's enzymes can reportedly produce ethanol from various feedstocks for around $1.35 a gallon. This is not yet competitive with existing ethanol production techniques, but if the company can continue to refine its process and its production capability or, alternatively, if it can find and patent new enzymes, its cellulosic ethanol could become competitive with other technologies in the near future. Furthermore, the fact that the company already has an operational facility and a commercial alliance with Shell give it a leg up on its competitors. In mid-2008, Shell increased its equity stake in the company to 50 percent.

WHAT TO WATCH FOR   The company's long-term plan is to license its enzymes to other ethanol producers. This is a unique business model, and it could serve the company well. Interested parties are encouraged to watch for news that other ethanol companies are, in fact, licensing its technology as well as monitor the status of the company's facility in Canada. At the present time its production is quite modest.

CONCLUSION   Neutral. The fact that the company already has an operational facility is a positive sign, as is its existing relationship with Royal Dutch Shell. Furthermore, in addition to playing in the ethanol field, Iogen is more diversified than many other ethanol companies in that its enzyme technology can also be used in the animal feed and paper industries. Nevertheless, the cellulosic ethanol field is in the midst of a serious consolidation, and it is not clear whether Iogen has the staying power to remain competitive. In 2008, it shipped a very modest 100,000 liters of ethanol to Shell. If the company considers an IPO, investors will want to see the company shipping at least 20–30 million gallons annually and know how it intends to multiply that figure by 2012.

COMPANY	Mascoma
INVESTORS	Khosla Ventures, General Catalyst Partners, Flagship Ventures, Kleiner Perkins Caufield & Byers, Vantage Point Ventures, Atlas Venture, General Motors, Marathon Oil, and Pinnacle Ventures
ADDRESS	161 First Street, Second Floor East, Cambridge, MA 02142
PHONE	717-234-0099
CEO	Bruce Jamerson
WEB	*www.mascoma.com*

DESCRIPTION   Mascoma is an early-stage cellulosic biomass-to-ethanol company using proprietary microorganisms and enzymes to produce cost-competitive cellulosic ethanol through a single-step method called Consolidated Bioprocessing. In 2009, it started a new company called Frontier Renewable resources to produce cellulosic ethanol in Michigan.

WHY IT IS DISRUPTIVE   Unlike Synthetic Genomics approach of creating cellulosic ethanol by manufacturing a synthetic cell from scratch, Mascoma is seeking to modify an existing microbe by adding desired genetic pathways from other organisms and disabling undesirable characteristics. The company is taking a two-pronged approach to the problem by either modifying an organism that naturally metabolizes cellulose to produce higher yields of ethanol from wood, straw, switchgrass, and other biomass or, alternatively, by engineering a bacteria that can live in high-temperature environments and whose only fermentation product is ethanol. If successful, Mascoma has the potential to produce cellulosic ethanol at a low cost from abundant feedstocks, which are readily available in most parts of the United States. In 2008, the company raised over $60 million in private equity, including sizeable investments from General Motors and Marathon, to help complete the construction of a modest-sized pilot project in New York State. The company also raised an additional $50 million in federal and state grants to build out a facility in northern Michigan.

WHAT TO WATCH FOR   Mascoma has already established key partnerships with a number of companies. It has an ongoing relationship with Genencor to produce enzymes that might efficiently breakdown lignocellulosic ethanol, and it has licensed yeast-based cellulosic technology from Royal Nedalco, a leading European Union ethanol technology company. More significantly, its relationships with Marathon Oil and GM suggest that if its plants in New York, Michigan, and Tennessee become operational, it will have the distribution network to ship its ethanol to the commercial marketplace. Before this can happen, however, the company must get those plants up and running at a commercial scale. The New York facility was originally supposed to be operational in 2008 but is currently only producing "demonstration-levels" of cellulosic ethanol.

CONCLUSION   Neutral. Until Mascoma's New York pilot project is fully operational (and producing in the neighborhood of 20 million gallons), it is difficult to assess the effectiveness of its technology. In general, cellulosic ethanol, while still a few years removed from becoming a mainstream technology, appears to have the potential to produce ethanol at a lower cost than corn-based ethanol. As such, it warrants investor attention. Nevertheless, Mascoma is just one of a handful of promising companies pursuing cellulosic ethanol. In the event the company goes public, you should review the status of Abengoa, Coskata, Iogen, Noyozymes, Poet, and Range Fuels' technology before considering an investment.

MBLX	COMPANY	Metabolix, Inc.
	SYMBOL	MBLX
	TRADING MARKET	Nasdaq
	ADDRESS	21 Erie Street, Cambridge, MA 02139
	PHONE	617-492-0505
	CEO	Richard Eno
	WEB	*www.metabolix.com*

DESCRIPTION   Metabolix is a biotechnology company dedicated to the development of alternatives to petrochemical-based plastics, fuels, and chemicals. Applying the tools of molecular biology, it has produced natural plastics that are biodegradable and have applications in packaging, consumer goods, and medical implants.

REASONS TO BE BULLISH

➤ Metabolix, in partnership with Archer Daniel Midland, formed Telles, a 50–50 joint venture to commercialize the production of *Mirel*—a natural plastic. By the end of 2009, the plant is expected to be producing 100 million pounds of natural plastic.

➤ *Mirel* can be used as an alternative to petroleum-based plastics in a variety of conversion processes, including injection molding, paper coating, and thermoforming. It can even be used as a material in medical implants and tissue engineering.

➤ *Mirel* is currently being used by Target Corporation for the plastic in its gift cards.

➤ The fact that *Mirel* is biodegradable in both composting units and sea water suggests it will appeal to environmentally conscious consumers as well as large corporations looking to improve their environmental image. If more cities and states follow San Francisco's lead and prohibit the use of nonbiodegradable plastics, Metabolix could be a prime beneficiary.

➤ Metabolix's plastic biodegrades without industrial composting or incineration.

➤ The global market for bioplastics is expected to grow 16 percent annually through 2012.

REASONS TO BE BEARISH

➤ At the time of publication, Metabolix was trading at just over half of its original IPO price of $14, and the company continues to burn through cash.

➤ The plastics industry, which historically has low margins, is not likely to embrace natural plastics until it is convinced they will be competitive in terms of costs and will perform to the specifications its customers have come to expect.

➤ Low oil prices will work against Mirel by keeping regular plastic inexpensive.

➤ Because Mirel is produced from corn it could get caught up in the food-versus-fuel debate.

➤ Metabolix will face competition from NatureWorks, LLC as well as larger plastics companies such as DuPont, Braskem, and Toray.

WHAT TO WATCH FOR If the Telles plant becomes operational in 2009 and Metabolix finds a market for all 100 million pounds of its natural plastic, investors can take that as a bullish indicator that the technology is meeting with widespread acceptance. Investors will also want to watch for signs that leading consumer companies such as Proctor & Gamble or McDonald's are requesting the plastic. In the meantime, you should monitor the company's success in using switchgrass as a feedstock. If successful this would go a long way toward negating the food-versus-fuel debate as well as give the company a low-cost, available feedstock. Longer term, if Metabolix can move into the medical market that would be a positive sign because it would open up the possibility of achieving higher margins on more specialized products. Also, if the U.S. Navy were to begin purchasing its plastic (because it is biodegradable at sea) that would be a bullish indicator.

CONCLUSION Bullish. The stock is currently trading at a fair price, and investors will want to make sure that the *Mirel* plant becomes operational in 2009. Even then, it could be a year or two before Metabolix sees any revenue from the deal. This is because Archer Daniel Midland made the upfront investment in the manufacturing facility, and it will receive the bulk of those revenues until its investment has been paid off. Nevertheless, with over 500 billion pounds of plastics consumed every year in America (accounting for nearly 10 percent of the total U.S. oil consumption), Metabolix could become a successful, long-term business if it can capture even a portion of this market.

COMPANY	NatureWorks, LLC
INVESTORS	Cargill
ADDRESS	15305 Minnetonka Boulevard, Minnetonka, MN 55435
PHONE	877-423-7659
CEO	Dennis McGrew
WEB	*www.nautreworksllc.com*

DESCRIPTION   NatureWorks is a joint venture between Cargill and Teijin Ltd. The company applies its proprietary technology to the processing of natural plant sugars to create a biodegradable and environmentally friendly polylactide acid, which is marketed under the brand of Ingeo. The bio-friendly plastic is being used in a variety of commercial products throughout the European Union and in the United States, including in Green Mountain Coffee Cups and Mrs. Field cookies.

WHY IT IS DISRUPTIVE   Because the plastics are derived from plants, it has been estimated that NatureWorks production process uses 65 percent fewer fossil fuel resources and emits 80–90 percent less greenhouse gas than traditional plastics. The company's plastic has also been certified as the first greenhouse-gas-neutral polymer on the market.

WHAT TO WATCH FOR   Being almost greenhouse gas neutral, NatureWorks would benefit from the imposition of any regulations limiting greenhouse gas emissions. Other factors likely to contribute to its growth are the development of improved polymers that can be used for a number of different applications. Those currently under development include natural plastics suitable for clothing as well as more durable plastics necessary for thermoplastic applications, including casings for mobile phones and computers.

CONCLUSION   Bullish. It has been estimated that biopolymers could reduce by 94 percent the amount of plastic consumer products that end up in local disposal facilities. And while it will likely be some time before such a goal is achieved, it speaks to the potential of NatureWorks' technology. In fact, the global market for bioplastics is expected to grow 16 percent annual through 2012. At this time, it is unlikely that Cargill would allow the company to go public, but in the event that it does I encourage you to consider an investment.

COMPANY	Poet Energy
INVESTORS	Private
ADDRESS	4615 Lewis Avenue, Sioux Falls, SD 57104
PHONE	605-965-2200
CEO	Jeff Broin
WEB	*www.poetenergy.com*

DESCRIPTION   Poet Energy is the largest dry mill ethanol producer in the United States. It currently manages twenty-three plants in five states and has another three under development. The company has been in the ethanol business for over twenty years and is highly specialized in the technological development, production, and marketing of ethanol. In 2008, unlike almost every other major ethanol company, Poet was actually able to increase production by 35 percent. As of 2009, the company was producing more than 1.3 billion gallons of ethanol annually. It has also recently formed a new division focused exclusively on biomass.

WHY IT IS DISRUPTIVE   In addition to its size, Poet is developing two different breakthrough technologies that are expected to help the company produce more ethanol with significantly less energy per bushel of corn. The first is its BPX technology, a patent-pending raw starch hydrolysis process that converts starch into sugar and then ferments without using any heat. This process not only reduces energy costs, but because it increases the protein content of ethanol co-products (primarily animal feed) it can also help increase the company's profit margins. The second technology is dubbed BFrac and separates the corn into three fractions: fiber, germ, and endosperm. The endosperm is converted into ethanol, and the other components are turned into higher-yield co-products. The real reason Poet represents a disruptive threat, however, centers on the company's ability to efficiently break down the complex sugar matrix found in corn stover and transform it into ethanol. The process appears to represents a real transition in the production of cellulosic ethanol, and its 125-million-gallon plant is expected to be operational by 2011. If it works as promised (and the company is now producing 20,000 gallons at a pilot facility in South Dakota), it could allow Poet to gain a

significant competitive advantage over those other companies that are just producing corn ethanol. To help aid the project, Poet has received a grant of up to
$80 million from the U.S. Department of Energy and another $15 million from the
state of Iowa.

WHAT TO WATCH FOR The cellulosic project is known as Project Liberty, and
company officials claim that it will be able to produce 11 percent more ethanol
from a bushel of corn, while using 83 percent less energy. If it can deliver on this
promise, Poet should remain one of the largest and most successful ethanol companies in America. The big question is whether ethanol from cellulosic sources
will be cost-competitive with corn kernels. Two other things that could work in
Poet's favor in the long run are the acquisition of ethanol plants from those producers that have gone bankrupt, and the federal government's recent decision to
increase the ethanol blend in regular gasoline above 10.21 percent. The mandate
will help create additional demand for ethanol.

CONCLUSION Bullish. Although Poet is a privately owned company and is not
available to individual investors, due to its size it is the type of company you need
to keep your eye on because it is likely to be one of the few ethanol companies
that will still be standing after the industry reaches maturity and many of the
smaller companies have either gone out of business or been acquired by the more
successful companies. In the event it does go public, revisit the status of Project
Liberty—and if it is successful—consider an investment.

Biofuel Companies

COMPANY	Range Fuels
INVESTORS	Khosla Ventures, Leaf Clean Energy, Blue Mountain, and others.
ADDRESS	11101 W. 120th Avenue, Suite 200, Bloomfield, CO 80021
PHONE	303-410-2100
CEO	David Aldous
WEB	*www.rangefuels.com*

DESCRIPTION   Range Fuels is a privately held company employing a proprietary thermochemical process, termed K2, to convert biomass to a synthetic gas and then convert the gas into ethanol. In 2007, the company received a sizeable $76 million grant from the U.S. Department of Energy to help build its first production facility. In 2008, it secured $100 million in private equity, and in 2009 it received an $80 million loan guarantee from the U.S. Department of Agriculture to help complete it cellulosic ethanol facility in Georgia.

WHY IT IS DISRUPTIVE   Range Fuels' technology is disruptive for a few reasons. First, like other cellulosic ethanol companies it holds the potential of being able to use a variety of agricultural products, other than corn, to manufacture ethanol. These include wood, switchgrass, corn cobs, and miscanthus grass. Secondly, the technology eliminates the uses of enzymes in the production of ethanol, and enzymes are an expensive component of traditional cellulosic ethanol production. Third, because the company makes cellulosic ethanol through anaerobic thermal conversion rather than fermentation or acid hydrolysis, the process converts the feedstock into ethanol at a significantly faster rate. As an added benefit, the process reportedly uses 15 percent less water, emits 60 percent less CO_2 than corn ethanol, and produces more ethanol per ton of biomass than other cellulosic processes. Finally, Range Fuels has developed a modular system that allows the company to place facilities near feedstocks (such as municipal waste sites or forest plants) as well as scale up production capacity quickly.

WHAT TO WATCH FOR   The company's lead funder believes that longer term (ten years), Range Fuels' technology can drive the price of ethanol production down to $1 a gallon. In the meantime, interested parties should watch to ensure the company meets its short-term goal of building a 100-million-gallon facility in Georgia by 2011 at a cost of $2 a gallon. Meanwhile, the establishment of additional production facilities in close proximity to various feedstocks will be a bullish sign that the company is moving in the right direction of meeting its other goal of producing 1 billion gallons of ethanol annually.

CONCLUSION   Neutral. The company is well funded and has an experienced management team. Provided Range Fuels' unique thermal conversion process works and it can deliver the cost advantages that company officials suggest, it is likely to be one of the few cellulosic ethanol start-ups to survive. Nevertheless, if the company goes public, interested parties should not consider an investment unless the company can document that its cellulosic ethanol is cost-competitive with other cellulosic ethanol producers.

COMPANY	Sapphire Energy
INVESTORS	Arch Venture Partners, Wellcome Trust, Venrock, and Cascade Investments.
ADDRESS	San Diego, CA
PHONE	858-768-4700
CEO	Jason Pyle
WEB	*www.sapphireenergy.com*

DESCRIPTION   Launched in 2007, Sapphire Energy is a relatively new start-up founded by a unique group of scientists, entrepreneurs, and investors. It seeks to create and grow genetically modified algae that will produce hydrocarbons. The company claims to have built a scientifically superior platform that uses photosynthetic microorganisms to convert sunlight and CO_2 into carbon neutral alternatives for conventional fossil fuels. To date the company has raised over $100 million to date.

WHY IT IS DISRUPTIVE   In essence, if Sapphire is successful, what the company will have created is the world's first renewable gasoline. It will also have created a new industrial category called *green crude production*. Sapphire's processes and final product differ significantly from other forms of biofuel because they are made solely from photosynthetic microorganisms, sunlight, and CO_2; are carbon neutral; and don't require any food crops or agricultural land (the algae is grown on large ponds using sunlight). In addition to circumventing the high input costs of other biofuel companies, Sapphire also avoids the food-versus-fuel debate. Moreover, because Sapphire's end product is gasoline (albeit renewable gasoline), the company's fuel can be streamlined directly into the world's existing oil and gasoline infrastructure. In mid-2008, the company announced its renewable ninety-one octane gasoline conformed to ASTM certifications, suggesting its fuel will also work in automobiles without the need to retrofit them. To understand Sapphire's upside potential it helps to remember that America imported over $200 billion of foreign oil in the past year.

WHAT TO WATCH FOR   Sapphire has publicly indicated it wants to raise $1 billion and be producing 1 million gallons of green gasoline by 2012–2014. This is an ambitious goal, and as of early 2009, the company had yet to achieve its initial production capability goal of 10,000 barrels per day. On the positive side, in late 2008, the company was selected by Continental Airlines to supply it with algae-based biofuel for the airline's first bio-fueled test flight. If the test flights are successful, it will be a bullish indicator that Sapphire is making progress toward its broader goal of becoming an oil company for the automotive market as well.

CONCLUSION   Neutral. The company has raised an impressive amount of money and is funded by some of America's most prestigious venture capital groups, but it will be difficult in the current economic climate to raise an additional $900 million to fund its aggressive build-out plans. Furthermore, it will be 2012 at the soonest before large-scale production begins, so Sapphire still has a good deal of time to mature. Finally, although the company's technology and process is unique, it must still compete with other algae-based producers such as GreenFuel and Solazyme.

COMPANY	Solazyme, Inc.
INVESTORS	Roda Group, Harris & Harris, Braemer Energy
	Ventures, and Lightspeed Venture Partners.
ADDRESS	561 Eccles Avenue, South San Francisco, CA 94080
PHONE	650-780-4777
CEO	Jonathon S. Wolfson
WEB	*www.solazyme.com*

DESCRIPTION   Solazyme is an early-stage development company working to synthetically evolve algae to produce a variety of valuable pharmaceutical, nutraceutical, and bioindustrial products (including biofuel) using genetic engineering methods.

WHY IT IS DISRUPTIVE   Because photosynthetic microbes require nothing more than sunlight, water, and inexpensive trace minerals, they are more preferable for the production of high-value molecules because of their lost cost and ease of use. In 2006, Solazyme received a grant from the federal government to pursue the development of a particular type of algae that might be able to produce biodiesel. To date, the project appears to be a success as the biodiesel is now being demonstrated in a limited number of automobiles. In 2008, the company signed a development and testing deal with Chevron and, in mid-2009, it secured an additional $57 million in venture-backed capital. A major lab also recently certified Solazyme's biofuel as ready to be tested in the jet-fuel market.

WHAT TO WATCH FOR   Solazyme is also producing algae that can create high-value molecules with utility in the nutraceutical and cosmetic industries. If Solazyme can successfully produce these products, it will help provide the company the necessary capital until its technology is mature enough to expand into the biofuel arena. In the meantime, it will be incumbent on the company to demonstrate that its production methods are commercially scalable. Longer term, it must prove its biofuel is cost-competitive with oil (probably in the $60–$80 a barrel range).

CONCLUSION   Bullish. Until the company creates a successful commercial product at a commercial scale, Solazyme remains a risky proposition. Nevertheless, its technology has a number of things working to its advantage (lower cost, ease of use). The fact that its fuel is now powering cars and that it has signed a testing deal with Chevron suggest there is great upside potential. In the event the company does go public, consider an investment but not before reviewing the status of competitors such as GreenFuel Technologies, Valcent Products, Sapphire, Solix, and Algenol. Investors are also advised to keep a close eye on Synthetic Genomics because its technology could render Solazyme's technology obsolete.

COMPANY	Synthetic Genomics
INVESTORS	Private
ADDRESS	11149 North Torrey Pines Road, La Jolla, CA 92037
PHONE	858-754-2900
CEO	Dr. J. Craig Venter
WEB	*www.syntheticgenomics.com*

DESCRIPTION   Founded by Craig Venter—one of the world's leading scientists and well recognized for his valuable contributions of sequencing and analyzing the human genome—Synthetic Genomics seeks to design, synthesize, and assemble specifically engineered cell-level biofactories that allow scientists to make extensive changes to the DNA of a chromosome, and insert it into an organism to perform very specific tasks.

WHY IT IS DISRUPTIVE   Essentially what Synthetic Genomics is seeking to create are "designer bacteria." The company begins by identifying the minimum set of genes necessary for an organism to survive in a controlled environment. It then creates the desired biological capabilities (which are found by sequencing the DNA of a wide variety of living organisms) and inserts DNA into the host. The latter is then placed into an environment that allows metabolic activity and replication. The 200-plus scientists working on behalf of the company have already developed one synthetic chromosome and are designing a proof of concept for two bioenergy applications—hydrogen and ethanol. If the technology works as promised, it could, quite literally, spark a biological industrial revolution by allowing living organisms to create ethanol and other biofuels by breaking down corn (or any number of other commodities) into a biofuel in one simple step. It is also possible that designer bacteria could be made to do a variety of other things. For instance, some believe that such organisms could be used for environmental remediation or perhaps even efficiently process carbon dioxide and remove the greenhouse gas from the environment. If successful this would be a major game changer. In mid-2009, the company agreed to a $600 million partnership with

Exxon to develop algae strains that will excel at sucking up greenhouse gases and secreting oil which can then be fed into refineries.

WHAT TO WATCH FOR   Interested parties are encouraged to closely monitor the status of the partnership with Exxon. Venter and his team have also been culling an unbelievable amount of genetic material from the world's oceans. It is possible that some of this new genetic information could be the key to creating highly efficient and effective biofactories. Company officials have indicated a breakthrough is possible within the next two to five years.

CONCLUSION   Bullish. Synthetic Genomics team of scientists have expertise in genomics, microbiology, human and evolutionary biology, bioinformatics, high-throughput DNA sequencing, environmental biology, information technology, biological energy, and synthetic biology. Each of these fields is experiencing near-exponential growth. To the extent the company can capitalize on this progress, it will only be a matter of time before such "designer bacteria" comes to fruition. Of course, there are still considerable technological risks, and Venter's confrontational management style is the subject of some concern, but at the present time, no other company appears close to achieving the goal of "designer bacteria." In the event the company goes public, risk-tolerant investors who can demonstrate some patience are encouraged to consider an investment. In late 2008, the company was named the number one private green company in the world by GoingGreen.

Biofuel Companies

VRNM	COMPANY	Verenium Corporation
	SYMBOL	VRNM
	TRADING MARKET	Nasdaq
	ADDRESS	55 Cambridge Parkway, 8th Floor, Cambridge, MA 02142
	PHONE	617-674-5300
	CEO	Carlos A. Rivas
	WEB	*www.celunol.com*

DESCRIPTION   Verenium specializes in the development of high-performance specialty enzymes, which have applications in the alternative fuels, industrial, and health and nutrition markets. Its technology is based on the metabolic engineering of microorganisms to more efficiently produce ethanol from a variety of different feedstocks including rice straw, corn stover, citrus pulp, and sugarcane.

REASONS TO BE BULLISH
➤ In February 2009, Verenium formed a 50–50 partnership with BP to commercialize cellulosic ethanol from nonfood feedstocks such as sugarcane and switchgrass.
➤ Verenium's technology is reportedly able to convert all of the sugar found in cellulosic biomass. This should allow the company to manufacture ethanol more economically than corn-based ethanol. In 2009, the company began the start-up phase at its demonstration plant.
➤ By supplying enzymes for processes other than the production of ethanol, Verenium has the added benefit of being more diversified than other ethanol companies.

REASONS TO BE BEARISH
➤ Verenium only has two modest-sized pilot projects under development: a 1.4-million-gallon pilot facility in Louisiana and a smaller plant in Osaka, Japan.
➤ The company is not profitable and might not be until 2011 or later. Also, it has only a small amount of cash on hand and a large amount of debt.

➤ If its demonstration facilities prove viable, the company will need to raise an additional $250–$300 million to finance the building of additional production capacity, but this will be difficult since credit has become tighter by the end of 2009.

➤ Verenium presently has a market capitalization of below $25 million and faces the real possibility of being delisted by Nasdaq in the near future.

WHAT TO WATCH FOR   Verenium's success will rest on its ability to get its two pilot plants producing at full capacity as soon as possible. You should then watch for news that the company has secured the financing necessary to build out its large joint venture facility in Florida. If it achieves these two things, look for the company to begin producing cellulosic ethanol in mid-2011.

CONCLUSION   Bearish. Until Verenium can demonstrate it is able to produce ethanol at a profit, investors are advised to stay away from the stock. Furthermore, the field of cellulosic ethanol is becoming very competitive. It is unlikely that all of the companies will be able to survive in their present form.

Conclusion

Among all the renewable energy categories—wind, solar, energy-efficiency—handicapping the biofuels area is the most difficult.

I see the industry breaking down in the following way. In the near term (2010–2011), corn ethanol will remain "king of the biofuels" and production will modestly increase as the "blend wall" increases. However, the industry will continue to undergo a major consolidation as larger and more efficient companies squeeze out smaller and less productive producers. Margins will remain razor thin and profits modest.

Around 2011–2012, cellulosic ethanol will appear on the scene and force another round of industry reorganization. Companies to watch include Abengoa, Range Fuels, Poet, and Mascoma. Over this same period, biodiesel will also grow in prominence, especially as a number of leading automotive companies begin introducing new lines of automobiles capable of being fueled by biodiesel.

Longer term the picture gets even fuzzier, but given the advances being made in the field of synthetic biology, investors are advised to watch companies such as Synthetic Genomics, Amyris Biotechnologies, Sapphire Energy, and GreenFuel Technologies because they could, quite literally, turn the biofuel industry on its head.

All told, the sectors near-term prospects remain poor and the longer-term picture is too muddy to do anything but place a very modest percentage of one's clean technology portfolio in biofuel companies.

"China is going to be a growth market but it's more of a 2011 story."

—Vishal Shar, Senior Analyst, Barclays Capital

Chapter Five

Solar: Cloudy Days Ahead or a Ray of Hope?

In the introduction to this chapter in the 2008 edition, I wrote: "Since 2004, the value of solar companies has soared from just under $1 billion to more than $67 billion. Such a rapid ascent naturally begs the question of whether solar is the 'next big thing' or merely this decade's equivalent of the Internet craze."

In the following year, the value of those solar companies soared to over $200 billion suggesting the field was the next big thing. Beginning in the fall of 2008, however, the solar industry shed all of those gains.

The bursting of the bubble may recall—and undoubtedly feels like to many investors—the bursting of the Internet bubble, but as I wrote at the time the comparison is not appropriate. First, unlike many Internet companies, all solar companies are manufacturing a tangible product. Second, and equally important, the solar industry is as much a victim of the global economic meltdown as it is a product of its own making (due to building an excess of capacity, which outstripped global demand). To this point, it is worth noting that even in the face of the tightening credit markets the solar industry actually grew its capacity by 1,265 MW in 2008. Total solar capacity in the United States now stands at 9,183 MW.

Who Will Be Left Standing When the Sun Comes Back Out?

All is not rosy in the world of solar, though. In addition to the financial markets drying up and causing companies such as BP to scrap a $97 million manufacturing facility and Evergreen to indefinitely postpone an $800 million manufacturing plant in China, some private solar companies, including OptiSolar, have had to fold up shop. Furthermore, in the race to meet growing demand in the first half of 2008, scores of companies ramped up production. As the financial markets seized up, not only did financing for the solar companies grind to a halt, it also made it difficult for their customers to purchase products. As a result, the supply-demand equation was flipped on its head, and in a matter of months, supply was outpacing demand by a wide margin. The net impact was to force prices between 25 and 50 percent lower.

The stormy conditions are having the inevitable effect of causing an industry-wide shakeout. As noted earlier, OptiSolar was forced out of business and was acquired by First Solar for $400 million in stock.

What is noteworthy is that the investors, who put $300 million in OptiSolar, were still able to walk away from the deal with more money than they had put into it. The reason is because what First Solar acquired was not just OptiSolar's technology and manufacturing capacity, but also a large 550 MW power purchase agreement the company had with PG&E.

The takeaway for investors is this: The less-competitive companies are unlikely to survive this economic recession, and the big fish are likely to get bigger.

A Ray of Hope

More significantly, the sea for these big fish will also continue to grow. In the fall of 2008, Congress extended the 30 percent Investment Tax Credit (ITC) for solar for eight more years. In February 2009, the president signed the American Economic Recovery Act and provided additional funding that will benefit the solar industry. Elsewhere, California modified its renewable energy standard to increase the amount of energy utilities must obtain from renewable energy sources from 20 percent to 33 percent by 2020; and, in China, the government announced a massive $585 billion economic stimulus package of its own—with renewable energy comprising a healthy part of that package.

Large deals are also still happening. In 2009, Southern Edison California signed the largest solar deal to date when it agreed to a 1,300 MW contract with BrightSource. Solyndra, another private start-up, has agreed to a series of large contracts with European Union providers. In the Middle East, a 10 MW photovoltaic system is being installed in Masdar City—the world's first carbon-free city; in China, the government has already initiated two solar projects (300 MW and 500 MW, respectively) under its "Golden Sun" economic stimulus initiative.

In the near term (through 2010), the majority of the solar industry's focus will remain centered on two things: improving the efficiency conversion rate of silicon solar cells and reducing the amount of silicon used in those cells. As to the former point, today most silicon solar cells—which represent between 90 and 95 percent of all solar cells currently sold—have an energy conversion rate of between 13 and 18 percent—meaning that only 13 to 18 percent of the sunlight that strikes a cell is actually converted into useable energy. A number of companies are dedicating a good deal of time, money, and effort to this cause, and you should monitor this area closely because a sizeable advance could cause a company to gain market share very quickly (and others to lose market share).

The second manner in which solar companies have been attempting to protect their margins is by creating economies of scale in their manufacturing processes. In the second half of 2009 the clouds over the industry began to part as Suntech Power, First Solar, and Trina all announced major expansions.

In many ways these two factors—improving the efficiency conversion rate and achieving economies of scale—favor the large solar manufacturers who have the resources, industry connections, and size necessary to achieve these goals. You should pay close attention to four of the largest solar companies: First Solar, Q-Cells, Suntech Power, and Trina, because they are likely to be formidable forces for the foreseeable future. As the industry shakes out in the years ahead and goes through a consolidation, look for many of these companies to be among those still standing.

Go Thin to Win?

In the interim (2011–2013), the dynamics of the industry may shift significantly. That is because new alternative solar technologies are on the verge of gaining widespread commercial acceptance. As mentioned earlier, silicon solar cells today comprise over 90 percent of the market. The remaining percentage is thin-film solar cells.

Typically these thin-film solar cells are made from strong light-absorbing materials such as cadmium telluride or copper indium gallium selenide (CIGS) and are much less expensive than their silicon counterparts because they don't use silicon. They also have the advantage of being amenable to large area deposition—a characteristic that enables them to be manufactured even less expensively because the cells are essentially sprayed onto the solar cells.

The downside to thin-film solar cells is twofold. First, thin-films don't currently last as long as silicon solar cells, and this means that they don't provide the same long-term payback as silicon solar cells. Second, and perhaps more important, they are not as energy efficient as silicon solar cells—meaning that thin-film solar cells must cover more space to produce a comparable amount of power. For many applications, such as powering a home or business, which has only a limited amount of space, this is an obvious disadvantage. But for other applications, such as large-scale solar farms, it is a nonissue.

What matters for these applications is the cost-per-watt of energy produced. Put another way, if a solar cell can be made large enough and at a low enough cost, even though it is not as long lasting or as efficient, it can still be more cost effective.

The thing investors need to keep a close eye on is whether thin-film producers can increase the efficiency of their cells while keeping their costs down. If they can, not only could thin-films become a more attractive option as a large-scale source of power, they could also begin replacing silicon solar cells for many uses. In fact, some analysts have suggested that the real question is no longer *if* thin-film solar cells can replace silicon cells but rather *when*.

To this end, I encourage you to monitor the work of those researchers who are experimenting with new cheaper and more abundant materials (such as iron pyrite) to replace cadmium telluride and CIGS, as well as the progress of companies (such as HelioVolt), which are attempting to incorporate solar cells directly into building materials. The effect of this advance is that labor costs for installation are eliminated entirely.

The competition won't end there. A number of private solar companies are also investigating promising new technologies and manufacturing techniques. For example, Konarka is seeking to coat nanoscale particles of titanium dioxide with light-absorbing dyes and incorporate those materials directly into polymers to create plastic solar cells. Nanosolar, another intriguing company, which has received over $300 million in venture capital funding, has devised a cocktail of alcohol and nanoscale compounds it claims it will be able to spray on a metal foil to produce flexible solar cells. These cells can then be manufactured in a roll-to-roll process. In late 2008, the company began construction of a manufacturing facility capable of producing 430 MW worth of solar energy a year. To understand the significance of this scale, it is worth noting that as recently as the year 2000 the entire manufacturing output of solar energy industry was just 500 MW.

Finally, it always remains possible that a different form of solar power—such solar thermal power or solar concentrators—will make a breakthrough that will change the competitive landscape.

In short, the clouds are lifting for the solar industry, and rays of sunshine abound. It is difficult to discern exactly where those rays of sun will land in the year ahead, but here's a look at some of the leading publicly traded and privately owned solar companies.

AMAT	COMPANY	Applied Materials
	SYMBOL	AMAT
	TRADING MARKET	Nasdaq
	ADDRESS	3050 Bowers Avenue, Santa Clara, CA 95052
	PHONE	408-727-5555
	CEO	Michael Splinter
	WEB	*www.appliedmaterials.com*

DESCRIPTION   Applied Materials is regarded as a "pick 'n shovel" investment play in the cleantech arena because it is now a supplier of thin-film deposition equipment. This equipment is expected to play a big role in facilitating the production of thin-film solar cells. In 2009, the company announced it intended to make a number of strategic investments in green technologies, including batteries, fuel cells, OLED lighting, and smart-grid technology.

REASONS TO BE BULLISH
➤ Moser Baer is building a large-scale, 250 MW thin-film production facility in India, and Applied Materials is supplying and installing the production line.
➤ In 2008, the company acquired Treviso, an Italian solar equipment maker.
➤ Applied Materials has made strategic investments in two promising cleantech companies, Fat Spaniel Technologies and Sage Electronics.
➤ To the extent the thin-film industry grows and comes to represent a larger percentage of all solar sales, Applied Materials is well positioned for growth.

REASONS TO BE BEARISH
➤ Profits were down dramatically in 2008 and the first part of 2009. The company laid off almost 14 percent of its workforce in early 2009.
➤ Applied Materials is primarily an equipment supplier for the semiconductor industry. Even if its thin-film solar business grows at a fast rate, it will still represent only 10 percent or so of the company's overall revenue. As such, it is important to remember the company's stock will remain more closely

aligned with the cyclical nature of the semiconductor industry than with the solar business.

➤ Many of Applied Materials customers cut down on production plans in light of the 2008–2009 recession. As long as credit remains tight, the company will find it difficult to grow.

➤ Silicon solar cells still dominante the solar market, and thin-film is likely to remain a niche market through 2010.

WHAT TO WATCH FOR   The pace of Applied Material's growth in the solar market will largely be determined by how quickly thin-film solar cell technology is adopted in the commercial marketplace. If advances in nanotechnology and plastic/polymer production are introduced in 2009 and 2010, it will be a positive sign for Applied Materials because such advances are expected to aid thin-film solar cell production. In the near term, watch for signs Applied Materials' customers are ramping up production, as well as for indications that the company is successfully reducing the price per watt of its solar cells to the $1.20 range. On the flip side, if its leading competitor, Oerlikon, is demonstrating success in these areas, it will be a bearish indicator.

CONCLUSION   Bullish. Applied Materials cannot be regarded as a pure cleantech investment, but if you're interested in adding some diversity to your portfolio or are intrigued at the prospect of adding a company with a relatively low price-to-earnings ratio, you should consider the stock.

ASTI	COMPANY	Ascent Solar Technologies, Inc.
	SYMBOL	ASTI
	TRADING MARKET	NASDAQ
	ADDRESS	8120 Shaffer Parkway, Littleton, CO 80127–4107
	PHONE	303-420-1141
	CEO	Farhad Moghadam
	WEB	*www.ascentsolartech.com*

DESCRIPTION   Ascent Solar is a development-stage company engaged in the production and commercialization of thin-film copper indium gallium di-selenide (CIGS) photovoltaic modules.

REASONS TO BE BULLISH

➤ The company has reportedly developed a process that will integrate solar cells directly into the building manufacturing process. If successful, the technology will allow the cells to come off the assembly line in the form of fully functioning solar modules. (It is likely that this labor-saving step will appeal to both homebuyers and building installers because the modules, which weigh about four pounds, will be able to be hand carried, and will thus reduce costs because no heavy operating equipment is necessary.) In mid-2009, the National Renewable Energy Lab certified its solar modules efficiency rate at 10.6 percent.

➤ The company has received one grant from the U.S. Department of Energy to help it increase the conversion efficiency of its solar cells to 20 percent, and another from the U.S. Air Force to develop a new material for inclusion in its solar cells.

➤ In 2009, Norsk Hydro acquired 35 percent of the company. The investment may be seen as a vote of confidence in Ascent's technology.

➤ Ascent is using the money from Norsk Hydro to begin construction of a 1.5 MW production facility.

REASONS TO BE BEARISH
➤ As a development-stage company, Ascent Solar is not yet profitable and is unlikely to be until 2011 at the earliest.

WHAT TO WATCH FOR   In the near term, I encourage you to monitor the status of Ascent's pilot production facility. It is expected to be producing 30 MW of modules by early 2010, and company officials have suggested that level could increase to 100 MW by 2011. Another promising indicator will be news that Ascent has increased the conversion efficiency of its cells to the 20 percent range.

CONCLUSION   Neutral. Ascent will likely be a volatile stock, and it is currently trading at a high price and unless it can successfully ramp up to commercial scale production levels it is more likely to go lower. Longer term, it is possible it could expand into the large and growing home- and business-construction market if it successfully integrates its solar technology directly into building materials.

CSIQ	COMPANY	Canadian Solar Inc.
	SYMBOL	CSIQ
	TRADING MARKET	Nasdaq
	ADDRESS	675 Cochrane Drive, East Tower
		6th Floor, Markham, ON I3R OB8 Canada
	PHONE	905-530-2334
	CEO	Dr. Shawn Qu
	WEB	*www.csisolar.com*

DESCRIPTION   In spite of its name, Canadian Solar is actually a Chinese company. (It is only incorporated in Canada; it does all of its manufacturing in China.) It is a vertically integrated manufacturer of mono and multicrystalline solar cells, solar modules, and custom-designed solar application products.

REASONS TO BE BULLISH

➤ The company has signed sales contracts for 262 MW of modules in 2009, with an additional 190 MW in the near-term pipeline.

➤ Its cash position is in the neighborhood of $130 million.

➤ The company recently opened a $10 million research and development center in China.

➤ In the event global demand picks up in the midterm, Canadian Solar has ample silicon supply agreements through 2015.

➤ Canadian Solar operates one of the largest silicon reclaiming business centers in the world. As a result, it has modest advantage over other solar competitors in that it has access to lower-cost silicon.

REASONS TO BE BEARISH

➤ For 2009, the company slashed its shipment outlook from 550 MW to 300 MW.

➤ Gross margins were negative for the final quarter of 2008.

➤ To date, the company has provided little information on the efficiency of its solar cells suggesting they are not as efficient as some of its other competitors.

WHAT TO WATCH FOR Any news that the company is shipping more than 300 MW of modules in 2009 will be a bullish indicator. If, however, the company further reduces its goal for 2009 and 2010, it'll be a bearish indicator. The company must also improve its margins. If its cash position continues to get smaller, it'll likely be viewed as an acquisition target.

CONCLUSION Neutral. Canadian Solar's stock has plummeted from $51 a share in mid-2008 to $20 in late 2009. The company remains financially solvent, but it will face considerable competitive pressure from larger and more established companies such as Suntech Power.

Solar Companies

DSTI	COMPANY	DayStar Technologies, Inc.
	SYMBOL	DSTI
	TRADING MARKET	Nasdaq
	ADDRESS	2972 Stender Way, Santa Clara, CA 95054
	PHONE	408-582-7100
	CEO	Stephen Deluca
	WEB	*www.daystartech.com*

DESCRIPTION   DayStar Technologies is engaged in the development, manufacturing, and marketing of copper indium gallium selenide (CIGS) thin-film solar cells. The company's main product, TerraFoil, has a stainless-steel base and can reportedly be integrated directly into such building construction materials as roofing and siding.

REASONS TO BE BULLISH

➤ DayStar is developing a next-generation product, which will reportedly have a conversation efficiency ratio as high as 10–11 percent.

REASONS TO BE BEARISH

➤ DayStar is generating little revenue and has a limited amount of cash on hand as well as a sizeable debt.

➤ The company has indicated it will use its money to construct a manufacturing facility in California to produce next-generation solar cells. To date, there is no indication that the plant will either be operational in 2009 (as promised) or that it will have the financial resources to expand if its technology and manufacturing process is successful. At a minimum, it appears DayStar will either need to secure a lot more money (and dilute existing shareholder value) or face bankruptcy.

➤ Even if the company's facility begins producing the next-generation solar cells, there is no guarantee that the product will be competitive with other thin-film solar cells being produced by such companies as Miasole, Solyndra, HelioVolt, or Nanosolar.

WHAT TO WATCH FOR   Investors need to monitor the company's cash burn rate. Second, the company has indicated that it plans to build a new facility capable of producing 25 MW of solar cells sometime in 2009. (A goal, which should be noted, replaces its earlier promise of having 50 MW of production capacity by 2008.) Until this facility is actually built and is producing solar cells with a conversation rate of at least 10 percent, investors are advised to stay away from this stock.

CONCLUSION   Bearish. A lack of money and a technology that appears to be inferior to those being developed by its CIGS competitors makes DayStar Technologies a very risky stock. If you're interested in thin-film solar cells, I encourage you to consider an investment in a more viable solar company such as First Solar; or, alternatively, wait to see if Miasole, HelioVolt, or Nanosolar goes public.

Solar Companies

ENER	COMPANY	Energy Conversion Devices
	SYMBOL	ENER
	TRADING MARKET	NASDAQ
	ADDRESS	2956 Waterview Drive, Rochester Hills, MI 48309
	PHONE	248-293-0440
	CEO	Mark D. Morelli
	WEB	*www.ovonic.com*

DESCRIPTION   Founded by Stanford Ovshinsky, Energy Conversion Devices invents, designs, develops, manufactures, and commercializes a variety of products for the alternative energy generation market, including thin-film solar cells, nickel metal hydride (NiMH) batteries, and fuel cell components. The company is organized into two divisions: United Solar Ovonics and Ovonics Materials.

REASONS TO BE BULLISH

➤ The company's revenues and profits have both been growing. In 2009, gross margins were 35 percent, and product sales were 51 percent higher. These figures are all the more impressive in light of the tough economy. The company's order book for 2009 is 100 percent full, and 2010 is already 50 percent full.

➤ ECD is well positioned to benefit from the U.S. government's push into renewable energy. The company is also growing in the French and Italian markets.

➤ In 2009, the company agreed to a multiyear agreement to supply Carlisle Energy Services with laminates.

➤ The United Solar Ovonics division is profitable, and because it employs a thin-film process that uses little polysilicon, its cells are less expensive to manufacture and install than traditional crystalline solar cells. As of 2009, the division produced over 238 MW of solar cells, and intends to increase to 420 MW by 2010.

➤ ECD owns 50 percent of Cobasys (Chevron owns the remaining half), which is the only U.S.-based manufacturer that offers NiMH battery systems for hybrid cars.

➤ The company has a very strong portfolio of intellectual property, and its management team has done an excellent job of forming constructive partnerships with leading corporations.

REASONS TO BE BEARISH

➤ Although sales are increasing and the company is ramping up production, it is doing so in the toughest economic environment in more than a generation. The company's profits could tumble in a severe or long-lasting recession.

➤ ECD's solar technology will face a great deal of competition from other solar companies, including First Solar and Q-Cells. If the price of silicon drops in the years ahead, the cost advantage of thin-film solar cells may fade away.

➤ To date, ECD has invested over $100 million in hydrogen systems but has little to show for its efforts.

➤ In the battery area, Toyota is using batteries from Panasonic. This suggests that Cobasys doesn't necessarily have a lock on the hybrid battery market. Other companies such as A123 are also developing competing battery technology.

WHAT TO WATCH FOR In the near term (2010–2011), the company's success will depend upon its ability to increase the margins on its solar business and ramp up production of its thin-film plant to a capacity of 420 MW. If it can achieve these things, the company will be well positioned to remain profitable. Longer term, you should monitor ECD's ability to continue to improve its NiMH battery technology as well as perfect its fuel cell technology.

CONCLUSION Bullish. In spite of the company's long history of unprofitability, the fact that its solar division is now profitable and growing suggests the company is headed in the right direction. Provided no other thin-film solar company (e.g., Nanosolar, Miasole, HelioVolt, or Suntech Power) develops a cheaper or more efficient solar cell, ECD is well positioned for future growth.

Solar Companies

SYM		
	COMPANY	Energy Innovations
	INVESTORS	Private
	ADDRESS	130 W. Union Street Pasadena, CA 91103
	PHONE	626-585-6900
	CEO	Joseph Budano
	WEB	*www.energyinnovations.com*

DESCRIPTION   Energy Innovations is a developmental-stage solar energy company. Its long-term goal is to develop solar systems that are cost-competitive with conventional energy sources.

WHY IT IS DISRUPTIVE   Unlike almost every other solar cell system—be it silicon-based or thin-film solar cells—Energy Innovations is attempting to construct its system out of an array of moveable mirrors that concentrate solar energy on a focused surface area. The advantage of the technology is twofold: First, it maximizes the energy it receives from the sun by getting more energy from a smaller number of solar cells. Second, by relying on a computerized system that moves the mirrors to match the angle of the sun, the system is able to stay productive later into the day (when businesses and homeowners are demanding the most energy).

WHAT TO WATCH FOR   The company installed its first 1.6 MW system at Google's corporate headquarters in 2007. It followed up on this success by installing a similar system at North Face corporate headquarters in 2008. It will need to demonstrate that it can build upon this success in North America and the European Union. Equally important, Energy Innovations will need to make good on its promise to deliver a solar system cheaper than its more conventional competitors. Unless the company can provide a shorter payback time for customers, it is unlikely that many businesses or homeowners will risk buying this newer technology.

CONCLUSION   Bullish. Although Energy Innovations has experienced a number of setbacks in bringing a product to market, the company has been usually open about its problems. But far from being failures, it appears the company is learning more about what is and isn't working. This bodes well for its future prospects because with each step it is getting closer to a practical product. To this end, the company recently secured UL certification for its SunFlower technology, suggesting it is safe and ready for the commercial marketplace. Energy Innovations is a private company and will likely remain so for some time, but you should be aware of the company because it has the potential to change how solar systems are manufactured.

Solar Companies

COMPANY	eSolar, Inc.
INVESTORS	Google, Idealab, and Oak Investments
ADDRESS	139 West Union St., Pasadena, CA 91103
PHONE	626-685-1810
CEO	Bill Gross
WEB	*www.esolar.com*

DESCRIPTION   Using proprietary technology in the form of small mirrors and software, eSolar uses anywhere between 24,000–100,000 mirrors to direct sunlight toward two water-filled heliostats (150-foot towers). The resulting heat creates steam, which drives an electricity-producing turbine.

WHY IT IS DISRUPTIVE   To date the company has raised over $130 million and has signed two large-scale power purchase agreements with Southern California Edison and NRG Energy for 245 MW and 500 MW. The advantage of eSolar's system is that the combination of small mirrors and software allows for the rapid and low-cost assembly of prefabricated modules, which can generate 33 MW of electricity. The benefit of this system is that it allows for the creation of big systems (such as the ones planned to supply Southern California Edison and NRG) to help utility companies meet renewable energy standards.

WHAT TO WATCH FOR   Before the company can begin supplying 245 MW and 500 MW of solar energy, it must first build the solar plants. (The company hopes to have the SCE facility operational by 2011 and to be producing at full capacity by 2013.) In addition to taking a great deal of money, which may prove difficult to come by in light of the credit crunch, the company must also receive all of the necessary permits to build and transmit its power. Overcoming these obstacles is no small feat. Beyond this, eSolar must prove its power is cost-competitive with other solar thermal providers such as Ausra and BrightSource Energy.

CONCLUSION   Neutral. Ausra, BrightSource Energy, Stirling Energy, and eSolar are all competing in the same arena, and it is too soon to know which company's technology will be the most commercially viable. Furthermore, in early 2009, eSolar licensed its technology to Acme, a large company in India, in return for a $30 million investment. On its face this might be appear to be a positive thing, but it suggests the company needs money and is willing to forego future profits (from the production of solar energy) in return for money today. If eSolar follows this path in other countries, it is relegating itself to becoming an equipment supplier rather than an energy producer.

Solar Companies

ESLR	COMPANY	Evergreen Solar
	SYMBOL	ESLR
	TRADING MARKET	Nasdaq
	ADDRESS	138 Bartlett Street, Marlboro, MA 01752
	PHONE	508-357-2221
	CEO	Richard M. Feldt
	WEB	*www.evergreensolar.com*

DESCRIPTION   Evergreen Solar develops, manufacturers, and markets solar power products through the use of its String Ribbon technology. String Ribbon is an efficient process for manufacturing crystalline silicon wafers. According to the company, it yields over twice as many solar cells per pound of silicon as conventional methods.

REASONS TO BE BULLISH

➤ Sales and revenue doubled for the year ending in 2008; due to a secondary offering, the company appears to have sufficient cash to weather tough economic times.

➤ Because the company's String Ribbon technology yields more solar cells per pound of silicon than conventional methods, Evergreen has less exposure to fluctuations in the price of silicon and is better positioned to maintain healthier operating margins.

➤ Evergreen Solar continues to improve upon its technology. The company's second generation 3.2-inch-wide ribbon has a 33 percent faster pulling speed, and this doubles furnace productivity. Future generations of the technology are expected to make further improvements in both speed and productivity.

➤ The company's Quad Ribbon wafer furnace promises further cost savings through lower material costs and reduced waste.

➤ Evergreen's strategic partnership, dubbed EverQ, with Q-Cells of Germany and Renewable Energy Corporation of Norway, positions the company well to compete in North America and the European Union.

REASONS TO BE BEARISH

➤ The company has yet to achieve an annual profit and is not expected to do so until 2011 at the earliest.

➤ Continued uncertainty surrounds the company's ability to secure additional financing and could threaten Evergreen's long-term expansion plans. To this end, the company recently began contracting out some of its manufacturing needs. In 2008, it postponed plans to begin construction of an $800 million manufacturing facility in China.

➤ Unlike some other solar companies, Evergreen does not have as much of its silicon under long-term contracts and while its technology uses less silicon than other methods it could still be vulnerable to increases in the price of silicon.

WHAT TO WATCH FOR   Evergreen will need to continue to focus on improving its technology, lowering its manufacturing costs, and increasing production capacity. If the company can continue to drop its price per watt from a present level of $2.65 to $1 by 2012–13 it will be a bullish indicator—as would signs that it is renewing plans for a manufacturing facility in Asia.

CONCLUSION   Bullish. The company will need to achieve extraordinary growth in order to become competitive, and its String Ribbon technology is vulnerable to advances in thin-film solar technology. But having dropped from $18 a share to $1, the company's stock now looks very attractive for investors with a higher tolerance of risk.

Solar Companies

FSLR	COMPANY	First Solar, Inc.
	SYMBOL	FSLR
	TRADING MARKET	NASDAQ
	ADDRESS	350 West Washington Boulevard Suite 600, Tempe, AZ 85281
	PHONE	602-414-9300
	CEO	Michael Ahearn
	WEB	*www.firstsolar.com*

DESCRIPTION   First Solar designs, manufactures, and sells solar modules. Unlike most other solar companies, First Solar manufactures its solar cells out of a polycrystalline thin-film structure that uses cadmium telluride (CdTe) semiconductor material to convert sunlight into electricity. The company is expected to reach 1.1 GW of capacity by late 2009—making it one of the world's largest solar manufacturers.

REASONS TO BE BULLISH

➤ First Solar increased its revenues by almost 150 percent in 2008, and its shipments grew by 140 percent.

➤ The company is currently manufacturing solar panels less expensively than any other solar company at $1 per watt, and its gross margins are the best in the solar business at 35 percent.

➤ In July 2009, First Solar, in partnership with EDF, announced plans to construct the largest solar manufacturing facility in France—capable of 100 MW annually.

➤ Because CdTe can be sprayed onto glass to create solar cells, it is significantly cheaper to manufacture than traditional silicon solar cells.

➤ CdTe has other benefits as well. It is less susceptible to temperature increases; absorbs low and diffuse light more efficiently than other materials; and, because it is a direct-bandgap semiconductor, the cells convert sunlight into electricity more efficiently than indirect bandgap materials.

➤ First Solar continues to make great progress in lowering the cost of manufacturing its solar cells. The company believes it will be able to lower the price below $1 per watt by 2010. (Conventional electricity costs in the neighborhood of seventy-five cents. Therefore, if First Solar continues to make progress, solar could be cost-competitive with fossil fuel sources as early as 2011.

➤ In 2009, the company acquired all of OptiSolar's projects for $400 million. This strategic acquisition gives the company a ready market to which it can provide its solar panels.

REASONS TO BE BEARISH

➤ At the time of publication, First Solar had a price-to-earnings ratio of 25 and had more than quadrupled in price from its original IPO price of $25. Even after its 2010 estimated earnings are factored in, the company is still trading at an extremely high forward P/E ratio.

➤ There is concern First Solar's inventory is growing due to slowing global demand.

➤ Although lower in price, First Solar's solar modules are not as efficient as silicon solar cells. If the price of silicon continues to drop, the company could lose some of its cost advantage.

➤ Spain, First Solar's largest market, has now capped its subsidies for solar, and the market is expected to contract by 80 percent in 2009.

➤ New thin-film technology could potentially replace First Solar's process as the lowest cost producer.

➤ First Solar may have overpaid for OptiSolar, and it might not be able to easily integrate all of the company's operations into its own.

WHAT TO WATCH FOR   First Solar will need to continue to lower the cost per watt of its solar modules. If it can reach a level between sixty-five cents and seventy-five cents per watt, this will be a major milestone and a bullish signal for the company—provided some other company such as United Solar Ovonics, Nanosolar, or Miasole doesn't reach this goal first. Investors should also watch for news that the company is continuing to make its solar cells more efficient than its current 10.6 percent efficiency level and that the company is expanding into new markets in the European Union and Asia.

CONCLUSION   Bullish. First Solar has a lofty price-to-earnings ratio, but its extraordinary growth can justify this valuation. If you have a higher tolerance for risk and a five- to ten-year outlook, you are encouraged to consider this stock as a long-term buy and hold.

Solar Companies

COMPANY	HelioVolt Corporation
INVESTORS	Sequel Venture Partners, Noventi Ventures, Passport Capital, Paladin Capital Group and Masdar Cleantech Fund
ADDRESS	8201 East Riverside Drive, Suite 600, Austin, TX 78744–1604
PHONE	512-767-6000
CEO	Ron Bernal (Interim)
WEB	*www.heliovolt.com*

DESCRIPTION   HelioVolt is a development-stage company seeking to apply thin-film photovoltaic coatings made out of copper indium gallium selenide (CIGS) directly onto building construction materials.

WHY IT IS DISRUPTIVE   Dubbed FASTT, HelioVolt proprietary process can reportedly produce layers that are 100 times thinner than existing silicon solar cells. Moreover, the process is said to be ten times faster than other thin-film processes. The technology can also print these solar coatings directly onto any number of substrates including steel, glass, and polymer. If true, this implies a number of building materials could double as solar cells. It would also remove many of the marginal costs typically associated with solar cells—such as converting the solar cells into solar modules and then installing those modules onto buildings. With HelioVolt's FASTT technology all of these costs would be eliminated because the building material is incorporated directly into the solar cell. The company's technology has received numerous awards and been recognized by *The Wall Street Journal* and *Time Magazine* as having one of the most promising technologies of this decade. The company has secured over $100 million in venture capital.

WHAT TO WATCH FOR   Nanosolar, Miasole, Solyndra, and others are also developing thin-film CIGS solar cells. To survive, HelioVolt will have to prove it can manufacture building materials coated with its technology. The company claims to be producing cells with a 12.2 percent conversion efficiency rate. To prosper,

HelioVolt will need to continue to improve this figure. The company's manufacturing facility is now operational, but it does not expect to ramp up to full capacity (20 MW) until 2010.

CONCLUSION   Neutral. HelioVolt appears to possess a disruptive technology. Until it can actually begin manufacturing materials at a commercial scale, however, it is just another company with a promising technology. If it successfully produces building materials that double as solar cells and is manufacturing 20 MW by 2010, you can expect the company to go public in 2011 or 2012. In the event it does, investors with a high tolerance for risk are encouraged to consider an investment in the company because it could change not only how solar cells are built but transform the building construction business by forcing builders to use photovoltaic building materials. Before taking such an action, however, I suggest you do your due diligence on HelioVolt's main CIGS competitors.

JASO	COMPANY	JA Solar
	SYMBOL	JASO
	TRADING MARKET	Nasdaq
	ADDRESS	No. 36 Jiang Chang San Road, Zhabei, Shanghai 200436
	PHONE	86-21-6095-5999
	CEO	Huaijin (Samuel) Yang
	WEB	*www.jasolar.com*

DESCRIPTION   JA Solar designs, sells, and manufactures monocrystalline solar cells primarily in China, although it also has customers in the European Union and the United States.

REASONS TO BE BULLISH

➤ Revenues continued to grow on a year-by-year basis from 2007 to 2008, and revenue is expected to continue to grow in 2009.

➤ In April 2009, the Chinese government announced a generous solar subsidy program. JA Solar, as a domestic company, is likely to receive a healthy share of the subsidies under this program—especially if the government institutes a domestic-production clause.

➤ JA Solar's parent company, the Jinglong Group, is China's largest maker of silicon wafers, providing the company secure and affordable access to this component of solar cells. This, in turn, should allow the company to post better operating margins than some of its leading competitors.

➤ In 2009, it signed a contract to supply BP with 175 MW of cells—and the amount could expand to 360 MW. It also agreed to supply 60 MW of cells to Solar Power.

➤ The quality of JA Solar's solar cells appears to be quite high and it offers a twenty-five-year warranty, which is attracting additional customers.

➤ The company's access to inexpensive Chinese labor should help keep its gross margins competitive.

REASONS TO BE BEARISH

➤ Although revenue is increasing, the company has reduced its projected revenues for 2009. The company could be left with too much inventory.

➤ JA Solar loaned 6.5 million shares to Lehman before the latter went bankrupt. The deal could severely hurt the company's ability to secure additional financing.

➤ The company only specializes in the production of solar cells. This practice could insulate the company somewhat from its customers and might hurt its ability to market its solar cells. Other competitors such as SunTech Power and Trina Solar are seeking to become more full-service providers.

WHAT TO WATCH FOR   Investors will want to look for evidence that JA Solar is improving the efficiency level of its solar cells in a range that will allow it to stay competitive with its peers. Investors will want to watch for signs the company is receiving a share of the new Chinese government subsidies and that it is also expanding beyond China and moving aggressively into the U.S. and the European Union markets.

CONCLUSION   Neutral. The company's access to silicon wafers through the Jinglong Group, in combination with its impressive operating margins and return on equity, suggest it is a company to be taken seriously. Moreover, as a Chinese company, it is well positioned to benefit from China's continued economic expansion and its growing commitment to developing clean energy sources. However, the solar market is likely to experience a good deal of consolidation in the coming years, and JA Solar has done little to distinguish itself from its more competitive peers.

COMPANY	Konarka Technologies
INVESTORS	Total, Draper Fisher Jurvetson, Zero Stage Capital, Chevron, Eastman Chemical, and numerous others.
ADDRESS	100 Foot of John Street, Booth Mill South, Third Floor, Suite 12, Lowell, MA 01852
PHONE	978-569-1400
CEO	Howard Berke
WEB	*www.konarkatech.com*

DESCRIPTION   Konarka uses nanomaterials and conductive polymers to manufacture light-activated power plastics, which are inexpensive, lightweight, flexible, and versatile. In 2009, the company received an additional $45 million from the venture capital market and a $5 million grant from the state of Massachusetts.

WHY IT IS DISRUPTIVE   Konarka is developing plastic rolls that can be embedded with titanium dioxide nanoparticles, which more efficiently convert natural and indoor light into electricity. In 2009, the National Renewable Energy Laboratory certified the company's solar technology at a 6.4 percent efficiency rating—the highest for an organic photovoltaic. The company's manufacturing process allows photoreactive materials to be printed or coated directly onto flexible substrates using roll-to-roll manufacturing—similar to how a newspaper is printed on large rolls of paper. The company first hopes to develop flexible solar coatings for laptop computers and mobile phones. Meanwhile, it is working on producing a solar tent for the U.S. Army that would produce its own energy. Longer term, it is working on inexpensive, lightweight rolls of solar cells that could cover the windows or building material of a home or business. Konarka's proprietary technology also offers a few other advantages over competitors' thin-film processes. For instance, its photovoltaic materials can be produced with different colors and varying degrees of translucency. This could enable the technology to be customized for new products and markets. The process also is environmentally friendly (no toxic solvents) and does not require manufacturers to buy or install any new equipment (it uses existing coating and printing technologies).

WHAT TO WATCH FOR   Dow, DuPont, BP Solar, Nanosolar, HelioVolt, First Solar, and Suntech Power are all working on related technologies, so there is no guarantee Konarka will develop the best or most practical product. The fact that it has partnerships with Chevron, Total (France's largest electrical utility company), and the U.S. Defense Department is a very promising sign. If computer laptop or cell phone manufacturers begin incorporating Konarka's technology into next-generation devices, or if the company enters into a partnership with a major manufacturer to produce solar shingles for roofs, it will be an even more bullish sign. The most positive indicator will, however, be Konarka's ability to decrease the cost of energy produced per watt. To this end, you should monitor the company's efforts at doubling the efficiency rate of its existing cells and improving its inkjet printing technology.

CONCLUSION   Bullish. Unlike most other thin-film solar companies, Konarka has an interim path to profitably if its solar cells can be used to supplement the power supply of existing mobile communication devices. Keep this company on your radar screen for a future IPO.

KYO	COMPANY	Kyocera Corporation
	SYMBOL	KYO
	TRADING MARKET	NYSE
	ADDRESS	6 Takeda Tobadono-cho, Fushimi-ku Kyoto, 612-8501, Japan
	PHONE	81-7-5604-3500
	CEO	Makoto Kawamura
	WEB	*www.kyocera.com*

DESCRIPTION   Kyocera Corp. is a large Japanese conglomerate that develops, manufactures, and sells telecommunications equipment and electronic components. It also owns Kyocera Solar, which is one of the world's largest vertically integrated producers and suppliers of solar energy products.

REASONS TO BE BULLISH

➤ In mid-2009, the company announced it was adding a 150 MW manufacturing facility in Tianjin City, China. The move will help ensure Kyocera remains competitive with low-cost manufacturers in the Asian market.

➤ Kyocera has four manufacturing facilities in Japan, China, and the Czech Republic. By the end of 2012, the four facilities are expected to be producing over 650 MW of solar cells.

➤ The company's multicrystalline silicon solar cells have achieved a new world record in efficiency by reaching an energy conversion rate of 18.5 percent.

➤ Kyocera is pursuing new markets for solar cells. One of the more promising fields is solar carports. The idea is to transform parking lots into mini solar farms, which can be used to reduce a company's energy bill while at the same time keeping employees' cars cool and shaded.

➤ In mid-2009, Kyocera Solar won a deal to supply Toyota with solar panels for the new Prius. The panels will only power fans to keep the interior of the car cool on hot days, but if they perform as promised it is possible they may power other internal electronic components in the future.

REASONS TO BE BEARISH

➤ The overwhelming majority of Kyocera's business is not focused on solar cells, but rather low-margin products such as black-and-white printers and low-end cell phones.

➤ As a Japanese company, its profits are sensitive to fluctuations in the exchange rate for the yen.

➤ Suntech Power and other Chinese solar manufacturers will have access to less expensive labor than Kyocera.

WHAT TO WATCH FOR   Kyocera Solar will need to continue to increase the efficiency of its solar cells as well as ramp up manufacturing capacity. Investors should look for news it has increased the energy conversion rate of its multicrystalline cells to 20 percent by 2010 and that it has ramped up its annual production to a capacity of at least 650 MW by 2012.

CONCLUSION   Bearish. Kyocera's core business of telecommunications and electronics does not stand out from its competitors, and Kyocera Solar faces too much competition from other solar manufacturers. If you're interested in a pure-play solar investment, you should consider First Solar or Suntech Power.

WFR	COMPANY	MEMC Electronic Materials Inc.
	SYMBOL	WFR
	TRADING MARKET	NASDAQ
	ADDRESS	501 Pearl Drive, St. Peter, MO 63376-0008
	PHONE	636-474-5000
	CEO	Ahmad Chatila
	WEB	*www.memc.com*

DESCRIPTION   MEMC is a global leader in the manufacture of silicon wafers and, although it primarily designs, manufactures, and provides wafers for the semiconductor industry, it is now supplying a growing percentage of its silicon wafers to the solar industry.

REASONS TO BE BULLISH

➤ In the first quarter of 2009 profits were $2 million as compared to a loss of $41 million over the same period in 2008.

➤ In late 2008, MEMC signed a ten-year silicon wafer supply agreement with Suntech.

➤ The company possesses over 500 patents and its granular silicon technology gives, it a price advantage over its competitors in supplying wafers to the solar market.

➤ MEMC has a strong balance sheet with over $1 billion cash on hand.

➤ Since avoiding bankruptcy in 2001, the company has made great strides in cost-cutting and streamlining its operations.

REASONS TO BE BEARISH

➤ Silicon is a basic commodity, and the industry has long been subject to boom/bust cycles. Since early 2008, the company has been in the midst of a severe bust. The company's operating margins are expected to decline from a high of 43 percent in 2008 to around 5 percent in 2009.

➤ MEMC faces a great competition from three other large silicon wafer suppliers.

➤ Although the company has ten-year agreements with Suntech and Conergy to supply the companies with wafers, it is possible the deals might fall through if silicon prices drop low enough. To this end, Conergy, which has already once renegotiated it contract down from $7 billion to $4 billion in late 2007, is currently suing MEMC in an effort to further renegotiate its contract.

WHAT TO WATCH FOR   Because the majority of MEMC's business is tied to the semiconductor industry, investors need to understand the cyclical nature of that business. Watch for signs that the wafer market is emerging from a period of overcapacity.

CONCLUSION   Bullish. MEMC is a well-managed, strong company. Given its steep stock price decline between 2008 and 2009 and the cyclical nature of the industries it serves, it is now possible its stock can gain appreciably—especially if government subsidies in the United States, China, and the European Union drive increased demand for solar cells.

COMPANY	Miasole
INVESTORS	Arcelor Mittal, Kleiner Perkins Caufield & Byers, VantagePoint Venture Partners, Firelake Strategic Technology Fund, Garage Technology Ventures, and Nippon Kouatsu Electric Co.
ADDRESS	2590 Walsh Avenue, Santa Clara, CA 95051
PHONE	408-919-5700
CEO	Joe Laia
WEB	*www.miasole.com*

DESCRIPTION   Miasole is a private solar start-up seeking developing thin-film polymer solar cells based on copper indium gallium selenide (CIGS).

WHY IT IS DISRUPTIVE   When combined in the right ratio, CIGS forms a direct bandgap semiconductor, which can be applied to thin-films in a unique roll-to-roll process that allows solar cells to be inexpensively printed on large plastic sheets. In addition to costing less per watt than traditional silicon solar cells, CIGS cells are efficient harvesters of photons in low-angle sunlight situations (such as at dawn and dusk) and low-light situations (cloudy days). Furthermore, CIGS cells are extremely lightweight, flexible, very stable, and reliant. In Miasole's case, its cells have a reported conversion rate of 10 percent. If true, its technology should gain widespread acceptance in the commercial marketplace. In 2007, Miasole was one of a handful of companies to receive funding ($20 million) from the U.S. Department of Energy to "develop high-volume manufacturing technologies and photovoltaic component technologies." The company has also received approximately $20 million from Arcelor Mittal in 2008 to pursue its manufacturing plans.

WHAT TO WATCH FOR   Miasole is competing directly with companies such as Nanosolar, HelioVolt, First Solar, Honda, Shell, and BP. Its success will rest on its ability to execute at the manufacturing level. To date there has been little evidence the company has been making much progress in this area. Making matters worse, since mid-2008, the company has replaced its CEO, and a key researcher left the company for a competitor.

CONCLUSION   Bearish. Until Miasole actually begins manufacturing solar cells at a commercial scale, investors should be very weary of this company. In the event it goes public, investors are encouraged to wait for signs of actual production before investing in this company. Better still, you should first ascertain when the company expects to become profitable.

COMPANY	Nanosolar
INVESTORS	EDF, AES Solar, Riverstone Holdings, Benchmark Capital, The Carlyle Group, Lone Pine Capital, Mohr Davidow Ventures, U.S. Venture Partners, Swiss RE, OnPoint Technologies, the Skoll Foundation, and Google's founders (Sergey Brin and Larry Page)
ADDRESS	2440 Embarcadero Way, Palo Alto, CA 94303-3313
PHONE	650-565-8891
CEO	Martin Roscheisen
WEB	*www.nanosolar.com*

DESCRIPTION   Nanosolar has developed and is producing nanowires and nanoparticles that allow it to "paint" the self-assembling nanomaterials onto flexible, low-cost sheets of plastic and convert them into photovoltaic cells.

WHY IT IS DISRUPTIVE   Traditional solar cells are manufactured out of silicon, which is costly, bulky, and inflexible. Nanosolar's technology offers the possibility that its cells will be a 1,000 times thinner and can be manufactured 100 times faster. The technology may even lend itself to being "painted" onto the sides of automobiles and buses. In 2008, the company received over $300 million to begin construction of two large-scale manufacturing facilities in San Jose, California, and Germany. It also received a $20 million grant from the U.S. Department of Energy to develop low-cost, scalable photovoltaic systems for rooftops. The company holds some valuable intellectual property from Sandia National Laboratories.

WHAT TO WATCH FOR   Company officials have claimed the manufacturing facilities in San Jose and Germany will be capable of producing 430 MW and 620 MW of solar modules annually, respectively. If true, this will represent a major paradigm shift in how solar cells are made. The plants were expected to be operational in 2009, but as of the publication of this book there has been no sign of a major ramp up. The company faces considerable competition from smaller, private start-ups (Miasole and HelioVolt) as well as larger more established companies such Q-Cells, First Solar, Suntech Power, General Electric, and Sharp (the largest manufacturer of silicon solar cells). If you are interested in future investment in Nanosolar, you will want to watch for evidence that the company is successfully reducing the cost of its solar panel toward the $1 a watt region.

CONCLUSION   Neutral. The company is currently not available to individual investors, but if it does go public, you should take a good look at where it stands in terms of meeting its ability to produce 1 GW of cells a year. Investors will also want to check on the status of its competitors' progress. If the former appears on track, risk-tolerant investors looking for a big payoff are encouraged to consider an investment.

QCE	COMPANY	Q-Cells AG
	SYMBOL	QCE
	TRADING MARKET	Frankfurt Stock Exchange
	ADDRESS	Guardianstrasse 16, Thalheim 06766, Germany
	PHONE	49-3494-66860
	CEO	Anton Milner
	WEB	*www.q-cells.com*

DESCRIPTION   Q-Cells AG is a German-based solar company engaged in the development, production, and sale of a wide variety of mono- and polycrystalline solar cells. It is the largest solar manufacturer in Germany and the second largest in the world.

REASONS TO BE BULLISH

➤ Since 1999, Q-Cells has been consistently profitable and growing rapidly. It produced 390 MW of solar modules in 2007 and increased that number to almost 575 MW by 2009. In 2009, in spite of a slowing global economy, it expects to increase that figure to 800 MW. The company's revenues, while not growing as fast as earlier projections, are still predicted to increase by 25 percent—from $1.6 billion to $2.1 billion—in 2009.

➤ Q-Cells has a long-term supply agreement with Elkem Solar to supply it with silicon through 2018. The contract calls for Q-Cells to receive a minimum of 2,400 tons annually with the right to increase the amount to 5,000 tons if necessary.

➤ Q-Cells sold its 17 percent stake in Renewable Energy Corporation (the world's largest manufacturer of polycrystalline silicon) in 2009, providing it cash as well as the ability to negotiate better supply agreements with REC.

➤ Of all the solar companies, Q-Cells is the most diversified in its approach to betting on next-generation solar technology. To this end, the company has acquired Solibro, a Swedish company commercializing copper indium gallium selenide (CIGS) thin-film technology. It is also investing in Brilliant 234 and

Calxyo (two companies producing silicon thin-film modules), and CSG Solar, an Australian company developing thin-film solar cells on glass.

➤ Sontor, a wholly owned subsidiary of Q-Cells, merged with SunFilm in 2009 to create one of the world's largest producers of thin-film solar modules. Q-Cells owns a 50 percent stake in the new company.

➤ In mid-2009, Q-Cells and LDK Solar formed a joint venture to develop large-scale solar plants.

REASONS TO BE BEARISH

➤ In the past year, customers have delayed and cancelled orders, and the company has twice had to lower revenue and sales projections.

➤ The company has benefited from the German government's generous subsidies to the solar industry. If these subsidies are reduced or eliminated it will have an adverse impact on the company.

➤ Like all solar companies, Q-Cells faces a good deal of competition, and it is possible that another company will develop a more efficient or less expensive solar module.

WHAT TO WATCH FOR   The company is performing admirably. Investors will want to make sure once its new production capacity comes online that its margins continue to improve. Investors will also want to watch for signals that Q-Cells is increasing the energy conversion rates of its existing product line of solar modules.

CONCLUSION   Bullish. Q-Cells has the right approach to prospering in the rapidly evolving solar market. While it has focused on increasing the production capacity of its existing silicon solar cells, the company is also placing bets on a wide variety of next-generation thin-film solar cell technologies in the expectation that at least one of these investments will pay off. If you are looking for a solid solar investment and/or want to add some foreign exposure to your portfolio, you should invest in this company.

Solar Companies

SOLF	COMPANY	Solarfun Power Holdings Co. LTD
	SYMBOL	SOLF
	TRADING MARKET	NASDAQ
	ADDRESS	666 Linyang Road, Qidong, Jiangsu Province, China 226200
	PHONE	86-513-8330-7688
	CEO	Harold Hoskens
	WEB	*www.solarfun.cn*

DESCRIPTION   Solarfun manufactures and sells monocrystalline and multicrystalline solar cells in China and the European Union.

REASONS TO BE BULLISH
➤ Solarfun has increased manufacturing capacity from 240 MW in 2007 to 360 MW in 2009.
➤ As a Chinese manufacturer, Solarfun is well positioned to benefit from the generous subsidy program the Chinese government announced in March 2009.
➤ In spite of the tough global economy, the company has been able to increase its gross margins over the past year.
➤ Solarfun has an agreement to sell Q-Cells a minimum of 100 MW of solar modules annually through 2011.
➤ The conversion efficiency of its cells is 16.8 percent, which is in line with industry averages.
➤ Solarfun has signed a long-term deal with LDK Solar to supply it with silicon.

REASONS TO BE BEARISH
➤ Although Solarfun's gross margins have improved, the company's sales declined 25 percent in 2009.
➤ Solarfun has sizeable debt and possesses little cash. If the global recession lingers, it may not be able to weather the storm.

➤ The company's CEO is expected to resign in late 2009, and a lack of leadership could hinder Solarfun during this critical period. Furthermore, over 50 percent of the company is owned by the founder, Lu Yonghua, and a large institutional investor, Good Energies.

➤ The company invests little in research and development, and it is not known whether it will be able to continue to increase the conversion rate of its solar cells at a pace necessary to stay competitive with others in the industry.

WHAT TO WATCH FOR   At a minimum, Solarfun will need to increase its manufacturing capacity and bolster the efficiency rate of its existing cells in order to stay competitive. Investors will want to make sure the company is nearing a capacity of 450 MW by the end of 2010 and that the efficiency level of its cells has increased to the neighborhood of 18 percent within the same period. The combination of the two factors may allow it to lower the cost per watt to a level that is competitive within the solar industry.

CONCLUSION   Bearish. It is unlikely all of the existing Chinese solar cell companies will be able to survive the almost inevitable industry shakeout. Little in Solarfun's literature suggests anything in either its manufacturing or technological capabilities will distinguish it from its larger and more established competitors. If you're interested in investing in a strong Chinese solar company, consider Suntech Power, JA Solar, or Trina Solar.

SWV	COMPANY	SolarWorld
	SYMBOL	SWV
	TRADING MARKET	Various European Stock Exchanges
	ADDRESS	Kurt-Schumacher-Str. 12-14, 53113 Bonn, Germany
	PHONE	49(0)228 559 20-0
	CEO	Frank Asbeck
	WEB	*www.solarworld.de.com*

DESCRIPTION   Established in 1999, SolarWorld became a major player in the solar industry when it acquired all of Royal Dutch Shell's crystalline silicon solar cell operations. It now bills itself as a fully integrated solar company that deals with everything from producing silicon to supplying solar modules, inverters, and solar roofs.

REASONS TO BE BULLISH
➤ In 2008 and the first half of 2009, the company reported a growth rate of 5 percent and increased revenues modestly—which, in an otherwise tight global market, bodes well.
➤ As a large company, SolarWorld can achieve the types of economies of scale necessary to be competitive. In 2008, it began production at North America's largest manufacturing facility, and in early 2009 it added additional capacity to the facility. By 2011, the company expects to be producing 500 MW of solar cells. With its close proximity to the California market, the company should be able to compete favorably in this area.

REASONS TO BE BEARISH
➤ SolarWorld remains focused on its crystalline silicon cells business. As such, it remains vulnerable to the prospect that thin-film photovoltaic cells will become increasingly accordable, more efficient, and more popular with customers.

➤ It will continue to face stiff competition from Kyocera, BP Solar, Suntech Power, and others.

WHAT TO WATCH FOR   Investors are encouraged to watch that SolarWorld maintains its strength in the Western European Union markets. You will also want to ensure that its planned 500 MW facility in the United States leads to additional sales in the North American market. Longer term, investors should watch for growth in the Asian market and, beyond that, a move into thin-film solar production

CONCLUSION   Bullish. SolarWorld has the potential to become one of the dominant players in the solar market and has done an excellent job of positioning itself for growth through 2011.

Solar Companies

COMPANY	Solyndra
INVESTORS	Argonaut Private Equity, ARTIS, CMEA Capital, Madrone Capital Partners, Masdar, Redpoint Ventures, Rockport Capital, and USVP
ADDRESS	47700 Kato Road, Fremont, CA 94538
PHONE	877-511-8436
CEO	Dr. Chris Gronet
WEB	*www.solyndra.com*

DESCRIPTION   Solyndra designs and manufacturers photovoltaic systems comprised of panels and mounting hardware for the commercial and industrial rooftop market. The company employs proprietary cylindrical modules and thin-film technology.

WHY IT IS DISRUPTIVE   Solyndra's cylindrical, thin-film PV panels are lined with tubes containing solar cells made of copper, indium, gallium, and selenide (CIGS) and are designed to capture optimal sunlight for a longer period of time than traditional flat panels. (An innovative white reflective roof coating reportedly allows the company to capture an additional 20 percent sunlight.) The company's 12–14 percent conversion efficiency, combined with lower manufacturing and installation costs, makes Solyndra's panels cost-competitive in the commercial marketplace. In the past year, the company has raised over $800 million in financing capital and, as of mid-2009, signed long-term distribution deals with EBITSCHHenergietechnik, U MWelt-Sonne-Energie, SunConnex, GeckoLogic, and Carlyle Construction Materials totaling over $1.8 billion. To help fulfill this large back order, the company received a $535 million loan guarantee from the U.S. Department of Energy to finance the construction of a 500 MW manufacturing facility.

WHAT TO WATCH FOR   Nanosolar, Miasole, HelioVolt, and others are developing competing thin-film CIGS solar cells. To prosper, Solyndra will have to continue to improve upon its 12–14 percent conversion efficiencies, as well as publicly disclose its production rate in order to ensure institutional investors it can meet its massive backlog orders.

CONCLUSION   Bullish. By virtue of its financial backing, loan guarantees, and established distribution deals, Solyndra appears to have everything in place to establish itself as one of the new leaders in the CIGS thin-film field. In the event the company goes public, you will want to consider an investment. Before doing so, however, it will be important that you verify the company is manufacturing modules at an annual rate of 500 MW or better and that an independent source has verified the company's claims of a conversion efficiency rate of between 12–14 percent.

Solar Companies

SPWRA	COMPANY	SunPower Corporation
	SYMBOL	SPWRA
	TRADING MARKET	NASDAQ
	ADDRESS	3939 North 1st Street, San Jose, CA 95134
	PHONE	408-240-5500
	CEO	Thomas H. Werner
	WEB	*www.sunpowercorp,com*

DESCRIPTION   SunPower Corporation designs, manufactures, and markets high-performance solar electric technology worldwide. Its high-efficiency solar cells are reported to generate 50 percent more power per unit area than conventional solar technologies, and its innovative tracking system allows the cells to better follow the sun throughout the day, also generating more energy. Sun-Power's cells' all-black appearance gives them a unique and attractive look that appeals to many customers.

REASONS TO BE BULLISH

➤ The company's unique tracking system and high-efficiency conversion rate allow its cells to generate more energy per square meter of space than any of its leading competitors. In fact, SunPower's new T5 solar cell roof reportedly doubles the energy generated per square meter.

➤ In 2009, the company, together with FPL, installed the largest solar farm (25 MW) in America. It is beginning a second project with Xcel Energy in Colorado and has also constructed the largest urban solar farm in America (in Chicago).

➤ In the past year, a number of leading companies, including Wal-Mart, Target, and Macy's, have selected SunPower to supply solar cells to their projects.

➤ SunPower has an adequate amount of cash on hand and a low level of debt.

REASONS TO BE BEARISH

➤ Sales are expected to decline almost 20 percent in 2009 and the company has already lowered revenue projections three times.

➤ SunPower faces stiff competition from First Solar, which is able to achieve lower costs through its more scalable manufacturing process, as well as from some of the Chinese lower-cost producers.

➤ Its success for the foreseeable future will remain closely tied to the continuation of generous government subsidies. Any decrease in the subsidies will have an adverse impact on its stock.

➤ At one time, SunPower was a subsidiary of Cypress Semiconductor. The parent company still holds a majority of the voting power on the board. It is possible that the board will not always act in the individual shareholders' best interest.

WHAT TO WATCH FOR The key to SunPower's success will be its ability to continue to increase the efficiency of its solar cells and decrease the amount of silicon used in the production of each cell. If it can continue to do this, the company and its stock should do well.

CONCLUSION Bullish. SunPower's stock has fallen from a high of $127 to $25 over the past year, making the stock attractively priced. The solar industry is likely to experience a good deal of consolidation over the next few years, but it is reasonable to expect SunPower to be one of the companies still standing at the end of the industry shakeout. The company's innovative technology, high-efficiency conversion level, and the aesthetic quality of its cells will continue to distinguish it from its other competitors.

Solar Companies

STP	COMPANY	Suntech Power
	SYMBOL	STP
	TRADING MARKET	NYSE
	ADDRESS	R & D Mansion 9 Xinhua Road, New District, Wuxi, Jiangsu Province, China 214028
	PHONE	86-510-8531-8888
	CEO	Dr. Zhengrong Shi
	WEB	*www.suntech-power.com*

DESCRIPTION   Suntech Power is engaged in the development, manufacturing, and marketing of photovoltaic cells and modules. As of 2009, it was one of the world's largest solar cell manufacturers.

REASONS TO BE BULLISH

➤ Suntech Power has been consistently profitable since 2003.

➤ Production capacity increased from 480 MW in 2007 to just over 1 GW in 2009. If necessary, Suntech can use this strength to undercut competitors' prices.

➤ In April 2009, the Chinese government announced a very generous solar subsidy program. Suntech Power, as a domestic company, is likely to receive a healthy share of the subsidies under this program—especially if the government institutes a domestic-production clause. To this end, the company announced in the summer of 2009 plans to begin construction of a 500 MW solar power plant under the auspices of the program.

➤ Because it is a China-based company, SunTech has access to lower manufacturing and labor costs than some of its international competitors.

➤ The company has acquired a minority stake in Shunda and signed a long-term contract with the company, which will supply it with silicon wafers through the year 2020. This means that a sizeable portion of its future silicon needs are guaranteed.

➤ In 2009, the company completed the largest grid-connected solar installation in China and also announced plans to begin construction on a manufacturing facility in the United States.

➤ The U.S government's stimulus package could benefit the company.

REASONS TO BE BEARISH

➤ Although the company has over 1 GW of production capacity, it is only producing at 60 percent capacity.

➤ Since the beginning of 2009, Suntech has had to cut its solar module prices by 25–30 percent, and the risk of continuing price wars remains a real possibility.

➤ The company's extraordinary growth has come at a cost. Its gross margins have fallen for the past few years, and the expansion of its manufacturing capacity has resulted in a sizeable debt.

➤ Silicon solar cells are now basically a commodity (meaning one company's solar cells are pretty much the same as another company's), and increased competition from major players such as First Solar and Q-Cells could squeeze Suntech's profits.

➤ Solar is still not cost-competitive with other energy sources without government subsidies.

WHAT TO WATCH FOR   If you're considering Suntech, you are encouraged to watch for four things: 1) Suntech's ability to increase the efficiency of its solar cells; 2) signs it is ramping up production of its low-cost Pluto technology solar modules; 3) indications that the manufacturing plant in the United States is proceeding according to plan; and 4) signs that the company is taking market share away from its smaller competitors such as Trina and SolarFun. As long as progress is made in these areas, Suntech will be competitive.

CONCLUSION   Bullish. Suntech has the ability to be the world's leading solar cell manufacturer. It has access to China's inexpensive labor and manufacturing capacity and an experienced management team. The fact that it is expanding its business in the United States bodes well for its midterm prospects (through 2012) and its strong presence in China will position it well for long-term growth.

Solar Companies

TSL	COMPANY	Trina Solar Ltd.
	SYMBOL	TSL
	TRADING MARKET	NYSE
	ADDRESS	No. 2 Tian He Road, Electronic Park, Changzhou, 213031, China
	PHONE	86-519-8548-2008
	CEO	Jifan Gao
	WEB	*www.trinasolar.com*

DESCRIPTION   Trina Solar manufactures monocrystalline ingots and wafers for use in its solar module production. Unlike many solar companies, it is vertically integrated and does everything from producing the silicon wafer to making and installing the modules.

REASONS TO BE BULLISH

➤ As a China-based manufacturer, Trina Solar has access to lower labor and manufacturing costs than many of its other competitors. Along with Suntech Power and Yingli Solar, it is regarded as one of the top three low-cost solar manufacturers. Its gross margins average around 23 percent.

➤ Trina will enjoy preferable treatment from its home government, especially as China seeks to bolster the amount of energy produced from solar power with the recent announcement of its generous subsidy program.

➤ Trina has secured a long-term deal with DC Chemical to supply it with polysilicon.

➤ It has entered into a strategic partnership with Q-Cells to supply that company with silicon wafers. The wafers, in turn, will be sold and marketed as Trina Solar modules.

➤ From a production level of 150 MW in 2007, the company is expected to increase to 550 MW by 2010.

➤ In the coming years, the company expects to triple its sales in the United States and tenfold in China.

➤ The average efficiency level of its existing solar cells is 16.3 percent, which is fairly competitive by industry standards.

REASONS TO BE BEARISH

➤ As a low-cost producer, Trina has little that distinguishes its products in the competitive marketplace other than price. If the price of polysilicon increases or a new disruptive technology undercuts it on price, Trina's stock will be hurt.

➤ The company has relatively little cash and a large long-term debt of approximately $450 million.

➤ Trina hasn't made much progress in improving the efficiency conversion rate of its cells. In the years ahead, it must demonstrate improvement or it will be a disadvantage to more aggressive competitors.

WHAT TO WATCH FOR   Trina must ramp up the production level of its manufacturing plant to 550 MW by 2010 to stay ahead of the game. If it falls short of this goal, it will be a bearish indicator. Investors are also encouraged to look for news that it is increasing the efficiency level of its cells beyond the 16 percent range and that it is gaining market share in the European Union, the United States, and China at the expense of higher-priced solar manufacturers.

CONCLUSION   Bullish. In spite of a quadrupling of its share price since the beginning of 2009, Trina is priced below its Chinese peers—Suntech Power and Yingli. If the company can make good on its promises to expand quickly in the U.S. and Chinese markets, it is a good long-term buy-and-hold stock.

YGE	COMPANY	Yingli Green Energy Ltd.
	SYMBOL	YGE
	TRADING MARKET	NYSE
	ADDRESS	No. 3055 Middle Fuxing Road, Baoding, China 071051
	PHONE	86-31-2310-0500
	CEO	Miao Liansheng
	WEB	*www.yinglisolar.com*

DESCRIPTION   Yingli Green Energy is a manufacturer of multicrystalline ingots and wafers for use in its solar module production. Unlike many solar companies, it is vertically integrated and does everything from producing the silicon wafer to making and installing the modules. Nearing 600 MW of production capacity, Yingli is now one of the largest Chinese solar manufacturers.

REASONS TO BE BULLISH

➤ As a China-based manufacturer, Yingli Green Energy has access to lower labor and manufacturing costs than many of its other competitors. Along with Suntech Power and Trina Solar, it is regarded as one of the top three low-cost solar manufacturers. It gross margins are currently around 15 percent, although it hopes to improve that figure to 24 percent in 2010.

➤ Yingli will enjoy preferable treatment from its home government, especially as China seeks to bolster the amount of energy produced from solar power with the recent announcement of its generous subsidy program. To this end, in July 2009, the company received a large subsidy from the Chinese government to build a 300 MW solar power plant.

➤ In 2009, the Longjitaihe Industry Group invested $627 million in a new joint venture with Yingli to make multicrystalline silicon solar cells.

➤ From a production level of 200 MW in 2007, the company is expected to increase that level to 600 MW by 2010.

➤ In the past year, the company has signed two large deals with IBC Solar and Goldbeck Solar to supply those companies with solar modules.

➤ In the face of tough macroeconomic conditions, Yingli appears to be one of the few Chinese solar companies that have survived relatively intact.

REASONS TO BE BEARISH

➤ Revenues for the first quarter of 2009 were down 43 percent over the fourth quarter of 2008, and gross margins had fallen from 24 percent to 15 percent.

➤ As a low-cost producer, Yingli has little that distinguishes its products other than price. If the price of polysilicon increases or a new disruptive technology undercuts it on price, Yingli's stock price will be hurt.

WHAT TO WATCH FOR   Yingli will need to ramp up the production level of its manufacturing plant to 600 MW by 2010 to stay ahead of the game. If it falls short of this goal, it will be a bearish indicator. Investors are also encouraged to look for news it is increasing the efficiency level of its cells beyond the 16 percent range, and it is gaining market share in the European Union, the United States, and China at the expense of higher-priced solar manufacturers. Investors are encouraged to pay especially close attention to the company's new N-type solar cell, dubbed *Panda*, which is reportedly capable of tripling the efficiency of its solar cells. If Yingli can pull this off it would be a bullish indicator.

CONCLUSION   Neutral. Its stock has quadrupled since the beginning of 2009 making Yingli expensive to its peers. If, however, the company can make good on its promise to increase the efficiency of its Panda module, it will be a good long-term buy-and-hold stock. Until such time as that news is announced, Trina and Suntech appear to be more solid investments.

Conclusion

If you are a patient long-term investor, solar represents a great area to search for some buy-and-hold opportunities. Yes, opponents are right to note that solar still accounts for only a miniscule one-tenth of 1 percent of the world's energy, but they are foolish to think that percentage won't grow handsomely in the years ahead.

Just consider the world of 150 years ago. America's leading source of oil came from whales, and the idea of deriving meaningful amounts of oil from the ground was dismissed as ludicrous. Of course, over a relatively short period between 1860 and 1880 the tables were reversed and it was whale oil that soon became an outdated relic.

Today, many energy experts matter-of-factly dismiss solar's potential and argue that only coal, natural gas, oil and gas, and nuclear power can possibly meet the world's energy needs. Perhaps they are right, but, personally, I believe it is worth investing in a few solar companies on the assumption that these experts might just be the successors to yesteryear's whale oil advocates.

To understand the opportunity from another perspective, consider this analogy: Imagine that on the first day of a month a single lily pad exists on a pond. Further imagine that the lily then doubles every day for the remainder of the month until the pond is covered on the final day of the month. On Day 20 of this little doubling exercise what percentage of the pond do you think is covered with lily pads?

Did you say one-tenth of 1 percent? Probably not, but that's the correct answer. Yet what happens over the course of the next ten days through the extraordinary power of exponential growth is really amazing. The percentage of the pond covered with lily pads grows from one-tenth of 1 percent to 100 percent!

Now solar power isn't growing exponentially, but it is growing rapidly. My point is this: Just because solar power is very small today (i.e., one-tenth of 1 percent) that does not imply it will always remain small. It is an opportunity the prudent, patient, long-term investor can exploit.

"Wind energy will be one of the most important contributors to meeting President Obama's target of generating 10 percent of our electricity with renewable sources by 2012."

—Stephen Chu, Secretary of Energy

Chapter Six

Wind Power: The Best of Times, the Worst of Times

"It was the best of times, it was the worst of times." So wrote Charles Dickens more than a century and a half ago. The same thinking could be applied to the wind industry as it approaches the year 2010.

From the more positive perspective, in 2008, installed wind power capacity in the United States increased 8,500 MW—or 50 percent—to 25,400 MW; in the first quarter of 2009, it grew another 2,800 MW to a total capacity of 28,200 MW. As a result, the United States has now surpassed Germany as the largest producer of wind power in the world.

In fact, wind power now produces enough electricity to power 7 million homes and, in 2008, it produced 42 percent of all new power capacity added in the United States. To understand how impressive this figure is, it helps to know that in 2004 wind power added a mere 2 percent of all new power. (Natural gas was then the primary source of new power.)

As impressive as this growth is, wind power still only generates 1.26 percent of America's electricity needs, and the growth rate is slowing—suggesting that the worst of times may be ahead. Furthermore, the industry is still overly reliant on governmental assistance.

Reflective of this slowdown, in July 2009 T. Boone Pickens cancelled a much heralded wind power project in Texas, while scores of other wind providers delayed orders and wind turbine companies laid off workers.

Three factors are responsible for the slowdown. First, the lingering global economic recession depressed the number of orders for wind turbines and the severe problems in the financial markets are making it difficult, if not impossible, for manufacturers to gain access to the capital necessary to finance their expansion plans. Second, the price of natural gas has fallen steeply. This has hurt wind power producers because power plants powered by natural gas are now more economical than wind-generated electricity. Third, the growth of wind power is being hindered by the lack of a modern transmission grid capable of transmitting the electricity generated by wind farms in rural areas to customers in more populated areas.

The question investors need to ask themselves is whether the proverbial glass is half empty or half full. From my perspective, the glass is half full, and I'm confident it will soon fill back up. For starters, on February 17, 2009, President Obama signed into law the American Recovery and Reinvestment Act. Among other things this extended by three years the production tax credit. This will have the effect of encouraging the production, purchase, and installation of wind turbines.

Meanwhile (2010–2011), the prospects are also favorable as it appears the Obama administration and Congress will pass a national renewable electricity standard mandating by a certain date that utilities receive a specified percentage of their power from renewable energy sources. At what level and by what date the legislation will stipulate is hard to determine. Nevertheless, legislation is likely to pass in 2010, and when it does, utilities across the country will look to wind power as a primary means of meeting the mandate.

Finally, it remains likely Congress will both enact some sort of cap and trade system regulating the emission of carbon dioxide and will appropriate a large sum of money for the construction of a "green superhighway" (updated transmission lines). The former will have the effect of making wind power more price competitive with coal and natural gas because it will place a tangible price on CO_2 emissions. The latter will help alleviate the issue of transmitting electricity generated by wind power from remote, rural areas.

More optimistic still, these governmental factors will likely be aided by continued advances in technological achievements. New composite materials and designs are making wind turbines more efficient and economical. Improved wind forecasting technologies and better demand-management tools are making it easier for utilities to rely on wind power as a stable source of energy, and advanced battery technology could help address some of the concerns over wind's intermittency problems. Together, all of these advances are lowering the cost of wind power. It has not yet achieved price parity with conventional sources of energy, such as coal, but it is getting closer.

The biggest factor fueling the industry's growth, however, is the simple fact that wind remains an abundant source of energy. The United States has been called the Saudi Arabia of wind power because of the vast amount of wind resources at its disposal. This is especially true if one takes into account the potential of offshore wind farms, which have been estimated to have the capacity to generate 900,000 MW of power. To understand the potential of wind power in America, it is worth noting that Denmark currently generates 20 percent of its power from wind, and Germany and Spain produce over 7 percent from wind. In short, from its current level of 1.26 percent, the United States has nowhere to go but up. The American Wind Energy Association, in fact, estimates that at current and expected growth rates the United States will be capable of generating 20 percent of its electricity in just a decade's time—by 2020.

This realization has caused an extraordinary number of European Union firms, which have been busily meeting demand in these European Union nations, to begin aggressively moving into the United States. In the past few years, Energias de Portugal, Vestas, Gamesa, BP, and Iberdrola have all added additional manufacturing facilities in America.

U.S. companies are not standing idly by. General Electric, which is now the world's largest supplier of wind turbines, continues to innovate and is presently working on constructing a new 3.6 MW turbine, which can be installed on offshore platforms to create massive wind farms. FPL Energy (a subsidiary of the FPL Group) has completed the construction of the largest wind farm in the United States—the 736 MW Hollow Horse facility in Texas.

All of this is important for investors because the biggest winners in the wind industry are likely to be these larger companies. This is because in spite of the claims of these smaller companies, the technological differences between most large turbines (1 MW to 3.6 MW) aren't significantly different from one another, so those companies that can achieve economies of scale in the manufacturing are likely to be the ones best positioned to achieve the type of margins that will allow them to remain profitable and grow the fastest.

This is not to imply that only large wind turbine manufacturers will be successful. This chapter will review a handful of the other smaller publicly traded wind companies that are attempting to carve out successful niches in the wind power sector.

CWP	COMPANY	Clipper Windpower
	SYMBOL	CWP
	TRADING MARKET	London Stock Exchange's Alternative Investment Market
	ADDRESS	6305 Carpinteria Avenue, Suite 300, Carpinteria, CA 93013
	PHONE	888-702-4663
	CEO	Douglas Pertz
	WEB	*www.clipperwind.com*

DESCRIPTION   Clipper Windpower is a rapidly growing wind energy technology, turbine manufacturing, and wind project development company. It has a large 215,000 square foot manufacturing facility in Cedar Rapids, Iowa, and has wind power projects in the United States, Mexico, and the European Union.

REASONS TO BE BULLISH

➤ Clipper is well positioned for growth. Revenues in 2008 jumped to $737 million from just $23 million the year before. Firm orders also increased to 289 turbines in 2008, and the numbers are expected to reach between 300–325 for 2009.

➤ In 2009, Clipper entered into a 50–50 joint venture with BP for the development of a 5,050 MW wind development project in South Dakota. As part of the long-term deal, Clipper will supply over 2,000 2.5 Liberty wind turbines and conduct the operation and maintenance on those turbines

➤ Also in 2009, Clipper signed deals with Electricia del Valle de Mexico and Colorado Springs Utility to provide those utility companies with enough turbines to supply 67 MW and 50 MW of wind energy, respectively.

➤ As more states adopt renewable energy standards, Clipper is well positioned to benefit from utility companies that look to purchase more wind power.

➤ Clipper invests heavily in research and development, and it possesses a strong intellectual property portfolio.

REASONS TO BE BEARISH

➤ Although sales have been increasing, the company reported a loss of $313 million in 2008—or $2.56 per share.

➤ Clipper is still reliant on the federal tax credit for wind development. If the credit is not extended, the company will be adversely affected.

➤ BP and Clipper's other clients have the right *not* to exercise options beyond their initial orders.

➤ Clipper faces considerable competition from larger and more established companies, including GE, Siemens, Vestas, Gamesa, and Mitsubishi.

WHAT TO WATCH FOR   If BP exercises its option to purchase additional wind turbines from Clipper and if the company continues to land other smaller deals, it will be a bullish indicator. Long-term investors will also want to keep an eye on the company's cash position and its ability to increase net margins as production increases.

CONCLUSION   Bullish. Clipper's relationships with larger energy companies such as FPL Energy and BP Alternative Energy are a positive indication that they are confident in Clippers technology and believe it possesses the ability to handle larger orders in the future.

Solar Companies

	COMPANY	EDP Renewables
EDPR.LS	SYMBOL	EDPR.LS
	TRADING MARKET	Lisbon Stock Exchange
	ADDRESS	Praca Marques De Gesta No. 2, Lisbon, Portugal, 1250-162
	PHONE	351-21-001-2500
	CEO	Antonio Mexia
	WEB	*www.edprenovaveis.com*

DESCRIPTION   EDP Renewables is one of the world's largest wind energy companies, and its majority shareholder is Energias de Portugal. In 2008, the company acquired Horizon Wind Energy and now has a large presence in the United States. In 2009, it acquired 85 percent of the Romanian wind power companies Renovatio Power and Cernavoda Power.

REASONS TO BE BULLISH

➤ EDP Renewables' wind generation jumped 40 percent in 2008 to 2,837 MW and its profits increased 87 percent in the first quarter of 2009.

➤ Its parent company, Energias de Portugal, is investing 75 percent of its project development budget ($4.2 billion) in wind-related projects and expects to have an installed capacity of 10,500 MW by 2013.

➤ With such a large portion of its electricity produced from renewable sources, EDP Renewables is well positioned to profit in the event the U.S. government imposes a cap on CO_2 emissions. The extension of tax credit for wind projects in the United States will benefit EDP immensely.

REASONS TO BE BEARISH

➤ As a foreign company, its shares will be exposed to fluctuations in the Euro exchange rate.

➤ The company is much smaller than some of its other European Union counterparts, and it will face considerable competition from Vestas and Gamesa in the European Union and the U.S. markets.

WHAT TO WATCH FOR   You should carefully monitor EDP Renewables' ability to digest its acquisition of Horizon Wind Energy and the two Romanian companies. If they are handled smoothly, the company's moves into the United States and Eastern European Union wind markets should pay healthy dividends.

CONCLUSION   Bullish. EDP Renewables is a fast growing company in a fast growing market. The extension of tax incentives in the United States is a big bonus and should keep the company on an upward trajectory through 2011. Moreover, its growing portfolio of wind resources makes it an especially attractive investment in the event governments around the world also impose strict limits on carbon dioxide emissions.

FPL	COMPANY	FPL Group
	SYMBOL	FPL
	TRADING MARKET	NYSE
	ADDRESS	700 Universe Boulevard, Juno Beach, FL 33408
	PHONE	561-694-4000
	CEO	Lewis Hay
	WEB	*www.FPLGroup.com* and *www.nexteraenergyresources.com*

DESCRIPTION   Through its various subsidiaries, FPL Group engages in the generation, transmission, distribution, and sale of electric energy. It generates approximately 37,000 MW of capacity, serves 4.5 million customers (primarily in Florida), and generated $16.6 billion in revenues in 2008. This makes it one of the largest utilities in the United States. However, it is its subsidiary, NextEra Energy (formerly FPL Energy), that makes FPL a cleantech investment. NextEra Energy is the largest owner of wind-power generated electricity in the United States.

REASONS TO BE BULLISH

➤ NextEra Energy is the world's leader in wind power generation and has over fifty wind facilities in fifteen states. In total, it generates over 6,375 MW of wind power. It also operates three of the five largest wind farms in America, including Horse Hollow, which, at 736 MW, is the largest wind farm in the country.

➤ Even in a tough economic climate, FPL, based largely on the growth of NextEra Energy, increased both revenues and profits in 2008 and the first half of 2009.

➤ In addition to wind power, FPL (through its operations at Solar Energy Generating Systems in California's Mojave Desert) is one of the largest generators of solar energy in the country. In 2009, FPL announced plans to construct three new solar facilities in Florida totaling 110 MW.

➤ The company currently benefits from generous state and federal tax credits for wind and solar facilities.

➤ It also has smaller stakes in two nuclear power plants and a hydroelectric facility in Maine. If the federal government imposes any restrictions on carbon dioxide emissions, FPL Group, as one of America's lowest carbon-emission energy producers, will be a clear winner.

REASONS TO BE BEARISH

➤ As a major utility subject to regulation, FPL is unlikely to generate exceptional returns.

➤ As one of the largest providers of electricity in Florida, the company is vulnerable to the damage that hurricanes can inflict on the region.

➤ NextEra Energy's parent company, FPL Group, is highly regulated within the state of Florida, and it is possible that regulators will not grant the company the type of rate increases management believes it needs to sustain its current level of profitability.

WHAT TO WATCH FOR   You will want to keep a close eye on the rates regulators approve for the company and the status of the federal tax credits—especially for wind power. If future rates increases are lower than expected or if the federal government reduces wind and solar power tax credits, it will be a bearish indicator.

CONCLUSION   Bullish. The fact that the population of the Southeastern United States is growing (which is where the bulk of the company's customers reside) suggests that future demand for FPL Group's electricity should remain strong, and given NextEra Energy's strong position in wind and solar power, the company looks to be a solid investment because the region's demand for both power sources should fuel future growth. Although it trades at a slight premium to its peers, investors looking for a conservative investment in the wind and solar industries would do well to consider FPL.

GAM.MC	COMPANY	Gamesa
	SYMBOL	GAM.MC
	TRADING MARKET	European Stock Exchange (Madrid)
	ADDRESS	Pol. Ind. Agustinos, C/A s/n, E-31013, Pamplona, Spain
	PHONE	34-948-3090-10
	CEO	Guillermo Ulacia
	WEB	*www.gamesavorp.com*

DESCRIPTION   Gamesa is engaged in the manufacture, supply, and installation of wind turbines and wind turbine generators. After General Electric, Siemens, Vestas, and Suzlon, it is the fifth-largest manufacturer of wind turbines in the world.

REASONS TO BE BULLISH

➤ The amount of wind power the company has installed has increased to 16,000 MW in 2009—an increase of 60 percent over 2007 figures.

➤ In 2008, Gamesa signed the wind sectors' largest ever transaction ($8.8 billion) with Spain's Iberdrola Renewables to supply it with enough turbines to provide 4,500 MW.

➤ In the same year, the company sold its solar power unit for $260 million to focus exclusively on wind power.

➤ In 2009, Gamesa agreed to supply a Mexican power company with five of its 2 MW wind turbines. It also agreed to supply 405 of its generators to China's Longyuan Electric Power Group. The deals suggest Gamesa is making good on its promise to become a globally diverse company. Its wind turbines are installed all over the world with 65 percent being located in the European Union; 12 percent in the United States; 10 percent in China; and the remaining 13 percent spread over the rest of the world.

REASONS TO BE BEARISH

➤ Gamesa will need to continue to demonstrate increased production capacity and improved productivity if it hopes to remain competitive with GE, Siemens, and Vestas. It also faces growing competitive pressure in China from such companies as Goldwind.

➤ The company experienced some manufacturing problems with its turbines in the past. The defects don't appear to be systemic but the problem does raise concerns about its quality control processes.

WHAT TO WATCH FOR   As the leading supplier of wind turbines to China, Gamesa has a great chance to grow its business. To this end, look for continued signs of expansion in both Asia and the United States.

CONCLUSION   Bullish. With over 16,000 MW of installed wind power, Gamesa currently possesses approximately 16 percent of the world market. Provided it can continue to increase its production, worker productivity, and its operating margins, the company will remain a solid, long-term investment.

COMPANY	Magenn Power
INVESTORS	Quercus Trust
ADDRESS	105 Schneider Road, Kanata, Ontario, K2K 1Y3, Canada
PHONE	613-599-0567
CEO	Pierre Rivard
WEB	*www.magenn.com*

DESCRIPTION   Magenn Power is an early-stage development company seeking to create a lighter-than-air tethered wind turbine that rotates about a horizontal axis in response to wind.

WHY IT IS DISRUPTIVE   If a prototype is developed as planned, company officials claim the system will be able to generate power with wind speeds as low as four miles an hour. This would be a substantial improvement over smaller stationary turbines that need wind levels to reach at least nine mph. A second potential advantage would be that because it can operate at heights of up to 1,000 feet—where the wind blows harder and with more frequency— the system should produce more energy than ground-based systems. Finally, because it is tethered, the system has great portability and can be moved in response to changing wind conditions. (This portability would also make it an ideal candidate for providing emergency back-up energy at disaster response sites.)

WHAT TO WATCH FOR   The company first needs to raise additional money, and then it needs to develop a prototype. The company expects to be producing its Magenn Air Rotor System (MARS) sometime in late 2009 or 2010. Until it can actually manufacture a commercial product, Magenn offers nothing other than a promising idea.

CONCLUSION   Bearish. Individual investors should stay away from this company. To repeat, it doesn't yet have an actual working product, nor does it have much money. It does, however, have a slick website and an effective public relations team that is good at getting stories about the company into the mainstream press. At this stage, you should leave the financing of this project to better funded and more risk-tolerant venture capital firms.

COMPANY	Southwest Windpower, Inc.
INVESTORS GE	Energy Financial Services, Chevron Technology Ventures, CTTV Investments, Altria, NGP Energy Technology Partners, Rockport Partners.
ADDRESS	1801 West Route 66, Flagstaff, AZ 86001
PHONE	928-779-9463
CEO	Frank Greco
WEB	*www.windenergy.com*

DESCRIPTION   Southwest Windpower manufactures and sells small wind turbines, including the Skystream 3.7, Air X, and Whisper Wind Turbines, for the home and small business market.

WHY IT IS DISRUPTIVE   The company's sleek Skystream 3.7 is a 1.8 kilowatt wind turbine that is extremely quiet (about the equivalent sound of an air conditioner) and works in low wind speeds. Moreover, it can be mounted on a pole no taller than thirty-three feet and needs only one-half acre to be sited. The device costs $5,400 (with installation between $12,000–$15,000); can power between 40 and 90 percent of a midsized, 2,000-square foot home; and will pay for itself in as little as five years. In 2009, the company received a big boost when the federal government granted a $4,000 tax credit for small wind turbines. As a result of this stimulus and growing demand in the European Union and China, where the company is now expanding, Southwest expects to grow between 90 and 100 percent in 2009 and is projecting profitability in the fourth quarter of the year. Among the dozen or so small wind turbine companies currently in existence, Southwest has been one of the most successful in raising venture capital and capturing the mainstream medias' attention.

WHAT TO WATCH FOR   Southwest Windpower will face competition from other companies focusing on the same niche, such as Bergey, BroadStar Wind Energy, and Mariah Power, so it will be important to keep track of developments within those companies. Beyond that, potential investors will want to monitor how well the company is doing in expanding into the industrial/commercial marketplace as well as penetrating the higher-income market of homeowners who can afford the technology and have the one-half acre of land to install the system. (It is estimated this potential market represents 13 million households.) One of the big hurdles Southwest will have to overcome is permit and zoning issues. Longer term, it is quite possible the company can develop a profitable market by selling its smaller turbines in China, the Middle East, and India. Efforts at expanding into these and other markets (e.g.;, South Korea) should also be monitored. Before these strategies are successful, the price tag on its turbines will have to come down.

CONCLUSION   Bullish. At the current time, Southwest Windpower's turbines are receiving a great deal of positive press, and it is likely that sales will continue to be brisk due to growing demand resulting from the generous U.S. federal government tax credit and growing international demand. However, to be successful in the long run, Southwest will need to continue to lower the cost of its technology. As the price drops, the economics of the turbines become more practical. In the event the company goes public, investors are encouraged to consider an investment.

	COMPANY	Suzlon Energy
SUZL.BO	SYMBOL	SUZL.BO
	TRADING MARKET	Bombay Stock Exchange
	ADDRESS	5th Floor Godrej Millennium 9, Koregaon Park Road, Pune 411 011, India
	PHONE	91-20-4012-2000
	CEO	Yulsi Tanti
	WEB	*www.suzlon.com*

DESCRIPTION   Suzlon Energy is the fifth-largest wind energy production company in the world and the largest in Asia. The company's services include manufacturing, operations and maintenance services, and consultancy services.

REASONS TO BE BULLISH

➤ Although Suzlon's growth rate has slowed over recent years, it was still able to manage 21 percent growth in revenues in 2008. Before-tax profits were also up 10 percent. As a result of new incentives for wind power by the Indian government, the company should be able to continue to grow.

➤ It is the largest supplier of wind turbines in India (the world's fourth-largest market), and it controls over 50 percent of the market in that country. By 2011, Suzlon expects to add an additional 1.5 GW of wind power. The company will likely continue to hold this position due to the very liberal tax incentives (80 percent depreciation in the first year and a ten-year tax holiday) the Indian government offers for all wind power purchases.

➤ The company's success is not limited to India. It has made significant inroads into the European Union, Australia, Brazil, South Korea, and the United States.

➤ Suzlon currently operates the two largest wind parks in Asia (Koyna and Vankusawade).

➤ In May of 2009, the company finalized its $1.7 billion acquisition of RE Energy and it is now an established leader in offshore wind turbine technology.

➤ As a vertically integrated company, Suzlon is positioned to capture profits from the complete wind power value chain.

REASONS TO BE BEARISH

➤ Over the past few years, Suzlon's wind turbine blades have suffered a series of high-profile failures. In addition to generating unfavorable press and hurting its stock price, the company has had to replace nearly 80 percent of the blades sold in the U.S. market.

➤ As a result of its acquisition of Repower, Suzlon has quadrupled its debt to $2.45 billion and has had to resort to selling some shares to generate the cash to pay for the deal.

➤ At the present time, Suzlon is still behind General Electric, Vestas, and Gamesa, and it will face considerable pressure from these companies as it seeks to bolster its place in the global marketplace.

WHAT TO WATCH FOR   The acquisition of Repower makes strategic sense, although investors need to monitor Suzlon's ability to successfully integrate the two companies. Investors are also encouraged to focus on Suzlon's ability to penetrate the Chinese market. Lastly, Suzlon must prove to the commercial marketplace that it has addressed the quality-control issues with its blades, which have plagued the company in the past.

CONCLUSION   Bullish. Since 2007, Suzlon has grown its share of the global wind market from 6 to 10 percent. Furthermore, as the dominant player in India, it is well positioned to consolidate its strength in that country, and its recent acquisitions in the European Union (RE Energy of Germany) make it a formidable player on that continent. Provided it can address its quality-control problems, Suzlon is well positioned to benefit from the global increase in demand for wind power over the coming years.

VWS	COMPANY	Vestas Wind Systems A/S
	SYMBOL	VWS
	TRADING MARKET	Copenhagen Stock Exchange
	ADDRESS	Alsvej 21, Randers, 8900, Denmark
	PHONE	45-9730-0000
	CEO	Ditlev Engel
	WEB	*www.vestas.com*

DESCRIPTION   Vestas Wind Systems is engaged in the development, manufacture, sale, marketing, and maintenance of wind power systems. It is the world's second-largest manufacturer of wind turbines and presently operates in sixty-three countries.

REASONS TO BE BULLISH

➤ As the world's second-largest manufacturer of wind turbines (after GE), Vestas is well positioned to benefit from the increase in global demand for wind power. Since 2007, revenues have grown from $6.2 billion to more than $9 billion.

➤ In 2009, Vestas announced plans to invest aggressively in the two fastest growing wind markets in the world—the United States and China. It will be investing $1 billion in the United States through 2010 and building three additional manufacturing plants. In China it will invest $365 million and recently began manufacturing a China-only wind turbine. The company also has production facilities in Australia, Denmark, England, Germany, India, Italy, Norway, Scotland, Spain, and Sweden.

➤ In 2009, Vestas signed major deals with Alliant Energy, E.On, and TransAlta to supply those companies with hundreds of wind turbines.

➤ The passage of economic stimulus packages in both the United States and China will benefit the company.

➤ As a supplier of both large (3.0 MW) wind turbines and smaller 850-kilowatt turbines, Vestas has the ability to handle midsized projects as well as large-scale projects.

➤ As the world leader in offshore wind turbines, Vestas is well positioned in this area. For example, China's onshore wind potential is 250 GW, but its off-shore potential is three times as large at 750 GW.

REASONS TO BE BEARISH

➤ In mid-2009, the company cut its projected annual growth from 40 percent to 20 percent.

➤ Vestas will face considerable pressure from GE, Siemens, Suzlon, and Goldwind.

WHAT TO WATCH FOR   The demand for wind turbines will increase for the foreseeable future. What potential investors need to watch for is whether Vestas can increase its future operating margins. Also, Vestas is still of such a modest size that it remains a possible acquisition candidate by a larger competitor.

CONCLUSION   Bullish. As one of the world's leading wind turbine manufacturers, Vestas is well positioned to benefit from the growing global demand for wind power. As of late 2009, its stock is trading at a healthy premium to its more diversified competitors (General Electric and Siemens). When its price-to-earnings ratio falls more in line with those companies, you should consider an investment.

002202	COMPANY	Xinjiang Goldwind Science & Technology
	SYMBOL	002202
	TRADING MARKET	Shenzhen Stock Exchange
	ADDRESS	No. 107 Shanghai Road, Urumqi, XNJ 830026, China
	PHONE	86-0991-376-7495
	CEO	Wu Gang
	WEB	*www.en.goldwind.cn*

DESCRIPTION   Xinjiang Goldwind Science & Technology is engaged in the development, manufacture, sale, marketing, and maintenance of mid- to large-size wind turbine generator systems. The company is among the world's top ten manufacturers of wind turbines and the largest in China.

REASONS TO BE BULLISH

➤ As China's largest manufacturer of wind turbine generators, Goldwind is well positioned to benefit from the increase in China's demand for wind power. By the end of 2010, China is expected to surpass the United States to become the largest wind power market in the world. Goldwind will benefit by virtue of its strong brand and first-mover advantage.

➤ Net profit in the first half of 2009 increased by 190 percent over 2008 figures, and the company captured 33 percent of the Chinese wind turbine market. In 2008, Goldwind sold over 3,500 turbines. The company has enjoyed annual growth of 100 percent for the past eight years.

➤ As one of three large Chinese wind turbine manufacturers, the company can expect to be a primary beneficiary of the country's large investments in renewable energy.

➤ In 2009, Goldwind signed a large blade supply agreement with LM Glasfiber and six other new sizeable contracts.

➤ As a supplier of both large (1.5 MW) wind turbines and smaller 600–750 kilowatt turbines, Goldwind has the ability to handle midsized projects as well as large-scale projects.

REASONS TO BE BEARISH

➤ Goldwind will face considerable pressure from GE, Siemens, Vestas, and Suzlon even in its home country of China.

➤ Since 2008, the company's stock has increased almost 400 percent. Investors buying now may be acquiring the stock at or near its peak.

WHAT TO WATCH FOR   The demand for wind turbines will increase for the foreseeable future. What you need to watch for is whether Goldwind's future growth potential and its ability to increase its future operating margins will continue to justify its inflated stock price. Other areas worth observing are Goldwind's progress in the development of larger (3 MW and 5 MW) turbines as well as its development of sea-based wind turbines. China has massive offshore wind resources, and if Goldwind can develop the technology to exploit this opportunity it will be a bullish indicator.

CONCLUSION   Neutral. As the China's leading wind turbine manufacturer, Goldwind is well positioned to benefit from the growing global demand for wind power. In China alone it is expected to triple in the coming decade. At the present time, however, financial information on the company is difficult to obtain, and after its recent price run-up, its stock is likely trading at a healthy premium to its more diversified competitors (General Electric and Siemens).

ZOLT	COMPANY	Zoltek Companies, Inc.
	SYMBOL	ZOLT
	TRADING MARKET	NASDAQ
	ADDRESS	3101 McKelvey Road St. Louis, MO 63044
	PHONE	314-291-5110
	CEO	Zsolt Rumy
	WEB	*www.zoltek.com*

DESCRIPTION   Zoltek Companies engages in the development, manufacture, and marketing of carbon fibers for various applications, including wind turbines.

REASONS TO BE BULLISH

➤ Because Zoltek's carbon fiber composites are lighter and more durable than fiberglass, the company's growth should match—if not exceed—the growth of the wind industry, which is expected to triple in the coming decade.

➤ The company signed a large deal to provide Vestas with $300 million worth of carbon fiber through 2012.

➤ BMW has explored the possibility of using the company's carbon fiber in the construction of its next-generation automobiles. If the entire car is manufactured with carbon fiber instead of steel, the weight of the automobile could be reduced 30 to 40 percent, and the improvement in fuel efficiency could be immense.

➤ In addition to servicing the wind and automotive markets, Zoltek's carbon fiber also has applications in the aerospace, marine, sporting goods, and oil and gas markets.

➤ Zoltek possess a low debt and should be able to weather the economic downturn.

REASONS TO BE BEARISH

➤ In the first half of 2009, the company's revenues were down 27 percent, and it barely made a profit.

➤ Zoltek has suffered in the past from concerns about its ability to meet customers' capacity needs. Until this shortcoming is addressed, large customers may be unwilling to commit to long-term supply deals.

➤ As the company grows it will need to raise sufficient funds for expansion. In addition to diluting existing shareholders, this expansion could push profitably out further into the future.

WHAT TO WATCH FOR   Zoltek needs to secure additional deals like the $300 million order from Vestas if possible. Another bullish indicator would be if the company opens a production facility in China to service that growing market. Lastly, investors will also want to closely monitor the project with BMW. If BMW (or any other automotive or aerospace company) announces that it will be using Zoltek's carbon fiber in a full line of its automobiles it will be a positive sign.

CONCLUSION   Neutral. Zoltek's stock is volatile, and it is currently trading at a relatively high price-to-earnings level, but the prospects for its future growth look promising. The company has little problem selling everything it manufactures, and the potential for additional growth should create a nice opportunity to increase its operating margins. As long as the wind industry continues to grow at 25 percent (or more) annually as expected, Zoltek should be able to ride the wave. The only danger is that as a smaller company it might not be able to handle such rapid growth.

Conclusion

Readers will note that the chapter listed just one Chinese wind turbine manufacturer, Goldwind. This is not because it is the only wind company in China; rather it is because the domestic Chinese wind industry remains small and fragmented. Nevertheless, surging demand has awakened both the Chinese government and domestic manufacturers to the industry's immense potential. And while most companies are not competitive at this time (most are still only manufacturing older "fixed pitch, constant speed" turbines), in the spring of 2009 the Chinese government announced its intention to invest heavily in the wind sector.

As this funding begins to yield advances, investors are encouraged to keep an eye open for the possibility of additional Chinese wind companies testing the public markets in the form of initial public offerings. If one or more companies does go public, you should give the companies serious consideration if, for no other reason, their access to low-cost labor will allow them to manufacture turbines for one-third less the cost of what U.S. and European Union companies can produce comparable turbines. Such an advantage in a large country with growing demand could result in the stock of one or more of the Chinese wind power companies experiencing healthy appreciation over the coming years.

"While there may not be a 'silver bullet' to meet the challenges of energy and climate change facing our nation, there are a lot of 'silver buckshot' technologies, which we can use to scale up and create an economically viable portfolio of energy choices."
— Vice Admiral Dennis McGinn, former Deputy Chief of Naval Operations

Chapter Seven

The "Alternative" Alternative Energies: Geothermal Energy, Fuel Cells, Wave Power, and Clean Coal

The previous three chapters focused on those renewable energy sources that have been attracting the most investor focus. Biofuels, wind power, and solar power are not the only renewable energy sources, however. There exist a handful of other options, and this chapter will focus on four of the most prominent: geothermal energy, fuel cell technology, marine power, and clean coal.

Because each energy source is so different this chapter will be structured somewhat differently than the earlier chapters. I will provide a brief introduction for each energy source and then profile those companies engaged in development of related technologies.

The Unknown Alternative Energy: Geothermal Energy

"The surge in new geothermal power development continues in the U.S."
—Karl Gawell, Executive Director, Geothermal Energy Association

It might be somewhat surprising to many people that geothermal energy—that is, using the heat from deep below the earth's surface to generate electricity—currently produces more energy than wind and solar power combined. Therefore, it is unfair to call geothermal energy an "alternative" alternative energy. It is more like the "unknown" alternative energy. But one of the reasons it is unknown is because as of 2009 it was producing only a scant 0.40 percent of the world's energy needs, and it was not growing at near the rates of wind, solar, and biomass energy production.

But like those other energy sources, it holds the potential to do a great deal more. A few years ago, a distinguished group of scientists released a report entitled *The Future of Geothermal Energy*. Among its key findings was that the United States could generate over 100,000 MW of electricity by 2050—or enough to power 80 million homes—if the federal government would make a serious commitment to geothermal energy research and development. The group estimated the price tag would be $1 billion.

More recently, the Geothermal Energy Association has identified new projects in the works and suggested U.S. geothermal capacity will soon double to 6,000 MW—or enough to power the three largest cities in California. Even more significantly, a U.S. Geological Survey report suggests geothermal energy has the potential to generate 530 GW of electricity in the United States. In the short term, 9 GW would come from conventional, identified geothermal systems and 30 GW from conventional, undiscovered geothermal resources. The vast remainder would come from unconventional and as yet undiscovered geothermal systems.

The potential of the latter sources is so extraordinary that it has been estimated that if the United States could tap into just 2 percent of the geothermal energy that resides between three and ten kilometers below the surface of the earth (and thus within the reach of today's drilling technology) it would be enough to supply more than 2,500 times the country's annual energy use.

Time will tell whether this potential is ever reached, but the current environment for the expansion of geothermal energy is looking up. In 2008, Congress extended the tax credit for geothermal energy and this will have the effect of encouraging the construction of additional geothermal facilities.

To this end, there are now fifty operational geothermal plants in the United States and another dozen (with a total capacity of 3,000 MW) under development.

The world's largest geothermal producer is Chevron. In the United States, Calpine Corporation operates the largest facility—the Geysers. Other companies include Ormat, Rasers, Western Geopowers, General Electric, Geodynamics, and most recently, Magna Energy, which filed for an IPO in July 2009.

The main consideration for investors contemplating an investment in geothermal energy is to understand that in the United States—and other places around the world—the upside is immense. To date, only a miniscule 3.5 percent of the geothermal base in the country has been tapped, and most of this activity has been centered in the western states of California, Nevada, Utah, and Hawaii where hot rocks are nearer to the surface and it is easier and less expensive to access them. As mapping and drilling technology continues to improve, so will the prospects for the field's growth.

The benefits of geothermal energy are extraordinary. Unlike coal and nuclear, it requires no external fuel source, and unlike wind and solar, it is not an intermittent source of energy. Geothermal plants don't emit any greenhouse gases, and they work around the clock. (Geothermal systems work by pumping water into the fractures around the hot rocks and then pumping that water back out in the form of steam. The steam then drives the turbines that generate the electricity.)

The one drawback of geothermal facilities, as previously mentioned, is that they are expensive to build and operate. Many experts, however, believe that they will soon be competitive in terms of price with other conventional energy sources, such as coal. For this reason alone, you should keep a close eye on the field.

CPN	COMPANY	Calpine Corporation
	SYMBOL	CPN
	TRADING MARKET	NYSE
	ADDRESS	717 Texas Avenue, Suite 100, Houston, TX 77002
	PHONE	713-830-2000
	CEO	Jack Fusco
	WEB	*www.capline.com*

DESCRIPTION   Calpine Corporation is a major U.S. power company delivering over 24,000 MW of clean electricity to customers in eighteen states. The majority of its electricity is generated from low-carbon, natural-gas-fired power plants. However, it also operates The Geysers—which is the largest geothermal facility in the United States and generates 750 MW of electricity through geothermal power. This makes Calpine the largest producer of geothermal power in the United States.

REASONS TO BE BULLISH

➤ In the event the federal government imposes restrictions on carbon dioxide emissions, Calpine is well positioned to benefit. Of the top twenty power generators in the United States, Calpine emits the least carbon dioxide. This is because the vast majority of its power comes from clean-burning, gas-fired power plants (which emit only 40 percent as much carbon dioxide as coal-fired plants), and its nineteen geothermal plants emit no carbon dioxide.

➤ The company emerged from bankruptcy proceedings in 2009, and it is now better positioned to grow in a responsible manner. In the first quarter of 2009, Calpine reported a $32 million profit as compared to a $214 million loss in the first quarter of 2008.

➤ Calpine has received widespread recognition from organizations such as the American Lung Association and the Sierra Club and is likely to maintain its image as one of the greenest power companies.

continued

Calpine Corporation continued

REASONS TO BE BEARISH

➤ As a result of the company's previous management team's decision to purchase too many natural-gas-fired plants before it could realistically begin servicing the debt on those plants, Calpine was forced to file for bankruptcy in 2005. As a result, the company is still burdened with high collateral costs.

➤ Calpine's stock increased more than 80 percent in the first half of 2009 and it is now priced high compared to many of its peers.

➤ Because the majority of Calpine's energy generation is related to natural gas—and not geothermal—it is subject to the volatile nature of natural gas prices.

WHAT TO WATCH FOR Investors will want to keep an eye on two things: 1) natural gas prices; and 2) Calpine's ability to identify and secure additional sources of land for the production of geothermal energy.

CONCLUSION Bullish. Calpine will remain one of the nation's largest energy producers and the cleanest (in terms of net carbon dioxide emissions). This will position the company well in the likely event the federal government imposes stricter limits on carbon dioxide emissions. At the current time, however, Calpine is trading at a premium. Long-term investors should wait until its price-to-earnings ratio falls more in line with that of its peers before considering an investment.

ORA	COMPANY	Ormat Technologies, Inc.
	SYMBOL	ORA
	TRADING MARKET	NYSE
	ADDRESS	6225 Neil Road, Suite 300, Reno, NV 89511-1136
	PHONE	775-356-9029
	CEO	Yehudit "Dita" Bronicki
	WEB	*www.ormat.com*

DESCRIPTION   Ormat Technologies and its subsidiaries are primarily engaged in the geothermal and energy recovery business. The company designs, builds, owns, and operates geothermal plants around the world. It also sells power units, including its Ormat Energy Converters, for recovered energy-based power generation. Ormat presently derives 73 percent of its revenue from the sale of electricity and 27 percent from the sale of equipment.

REASONS TO BE BULLISH

➤ In 2009, Ormat signed large deals to build geothermal power plants in New Zealand, Kenya, Turkey, and Costa Rica. The deals in New Zealand, Turkey, and Kenya were repeat orders suggesting the host countries are pleased with Ormat's technology.

➤ In the first quarter of 2009, the company reported a profit of $14.6 million, and the passage of renewable tax credit legislation in October 2008 in the United States bodes well for Ormat's future growth.

➤ Ormat has recently acquired large geothermal rights in Alaska, California, and Nevada.

➤ Because its geothermal facilities don't produce any greenhouse gases, in the event the federal government imposes a cost on carbon dioxide and nitrogen oxide (NOx) emissions, Ormat will thrive in this stricter regulatory environment.

continued

Ormat Technologies, Inc. continued

➤ By reinjecting 100 percent of the geothermal fluid back into its systems, the company's Energy Recovery units conserve resources and save money.
➤ Ormat's technology is suitable for projects as small as 250 KW. This trait and the fact that its technology is modular in nature give the company the ability to incrementally expand its geothermal facilities. This not only reduces the risk for Ormat customers but provides the company a way to grow with its customers.

REASONS TO BE BEARISH

➤ In 2008, the company reported slower-than-expected growth due to higher-than-expected material costs, plant outages, and high maintenance costs at its new facilities. Future facilities could experience similar cost overruns.
➤ Ormat bears some risk when it acquires geothermal rights because the cost of exploration is extremely high. Furthermore, even if the site is suitable, often its location is far from urban areas (and thus electricity users) and the cost of transmitting the energy over the existing grid is high. If alternative renewable energy sources such as thin-film solar farms become economical, Ormat's large-scale and expensive geothermal facilities could be at an economic disadvantage.
➤ The company's presence in foreign markets makes it vulnerable to currency fluctuations.

WHAT TO WATCH FOR You will want to continue to monitor for signs that Ormat is signing contracts to build geothermal facilities around the world. Next, pay close attention to whether the geothermal rights in Alaska, California, and Nevada can be developed at a reasonable cost. Finally, the U.S. government's continued support for geothermal power in the form of research and development expenditures and tax credits will be important for Ormat's future success.

CONCLUSION Bullish. As both a supplier of clean energy technology and a seller of much of the electricity it produces, Ormat is well positioned to benefit from the growth of geothermal energy. It is the closest thing to a pure-play in the geothermal arena. Furthermore, because its geothermal units are modular in nature, the company can start by manufacturing smaller facilities and adding to those facilities as its customer's energy need to grow.

Alternative Energy Companies

RZ	COMPANY	Raser Technologies, Inc.
	SYMBOL	RZ
	TRADING MARKET	NYSE
	ADDRESS	5152 North Edgewood Drive, Suite 375, Provo, UT 84604
	PHONE	801-765-1200
	CEO	Brent Cook
	WEB	*www.rasertech.com*

DESCRIPTION Raser Technologies bills itself as a "technology licensing and development" company. It operates two segments: 1) transportation and industrial technology and 2) power systems. The former is focused on improving the power density and efficiency of electric motors. The latter develops geothermal electric power generating plants and bottom-cycling operations, which generate electric power from existing power plants. The company calls this dual focus a *well-to-wheel strategy* because it believes it will be able to generate electricity from geothermal power (the well) and then transmit that power to vehicles (the wheel). Raser has also accumulated a portfolio of geothermal interests in the United States and Indonesia.

REASONS TO BE BULLISH

➤ In late 2007, Raser began operation of its first geothermal plant in Beaver County, Utah, and the plant is supplying energy to 18,000 homes in Anaheim, California.

➤ The company has signed a similar deal with the Salt River Power District (which supplies energy to the Phoenix, Arizona, area).

➤ In 2008, Raser signed a deal with PG&E to supply it with two SUVs, which employ its electric motor technology.

REASONS TO BE BEARISH

➤ Raser reported a dismal $41,000 in revenues for the first quarter of 2009 and has only $159,000 cash on hand. This compares with a debt of almost $90 million. The company is also burning money at an unsustainable rate. Worse, most of the money is going to general administrative costs and not research and development.

➤ Raser faces a great deal of competition in both the production of electric motors and geothermal power production.

WHAT TO WATCH FOR The company claims to want to produce approximately 100 MW of new geothermal energy each year for the next five years. To do so, it will need to secure additional land leases; arrange the necessary financing; line up new customers; and, of course, build the plants to generate the energy. It is a tall order to fill with such a weak balance sheet.

CONCLUSION Bearish. At the present time, Raser is generating little in the way of revenues but is sporting a market capitalization of $145 million. Nothing in either the company's technology or strategy (short of actually building large-scale geothermal plants capable of generating 100 MW-plus of electrical power) justifies this type of valuation. The plant to supply Anaheim is a start, but the company will need to do a lot more to justify its inflated stock price. Because of the company's cash burn rate it will soon need to raise additional money. When it does, existing shareholders can expect to have their stock further diluted. If you're interested in geothermal power, consider Ormat Technologies as a more viable investment.

WGP.V	COMPANY	Western Geopower
	SYMBOL	WGP.V
	TRADING MARKET	TSX Venture Exchange—Vancouver
	ADDRESS	409 Granville Street, Suite 400, Vancouver, Canada V6C 1T2
	PHONE	604-662-3338
	CEO	Kenneth MacLeod
	WEB	*www.geopower.ca*

DESCRIPTION Western Geopower is a renewable energy company dedicated to the development of geothermal energy projects for the delivery of clean power. The company holds 100 percent interest in the Unit 15 Steam Field located in the Geysers Geothermal Field in California. It is also developing Canada's most viable geothermal field—the South Meager Geothermal Project in British Columbia.

REASONS TO BE BULLISH

➤ In 2008, the company signed a power purchase agreement to deliver 265,000 MW per year of geothermal power to the Northern California Power Agency. The deal is expected to generate $26 million in revenue annually over the twenty-year life of the contract.

➤ As a result of the California state legislature's decision to mandate utilities to purchase a minimum of 20 percent of their electricity from renewable energy sources by 2010, Western Geopower is well positioned to benefit.

➤ If the company's South Meager Field project is found to be viable, the company will be similarly suited to supply clean power to utilities in Canada.

➤ Western Geothermal secured an additional $25 million in 2008 to pursue the development of the South Meager project.

REASONS TO BE BEARISH

➤ Western Geopower is currently losing money and will likely continue to operate at a loss until the South Meager Field geothermal facility is operating at full capacity.

➤ Since the price of oil and natural gas has plummeted in the past year, geothermal energy is looking less attractive from a price-comparison perspective.

➤ The company only began being traded as a publicly held company in late 2006, and it did so in order to finance its project in The Geysers. Because geothermal facilities are expensive to build and operate, it is possible that the company will need to issue additional shares in the near future to raise more money. This could have the effect of diluting the value of existing shareholders' stock.

➤ Western Geopower will face competition from both Calpine Corporation and Ormat in the California market, and Magma Energy in the Canadian market.

WHAT TO WATCH FOR The success of Western Geopower will hinge on its ability to get the South Meager facility operational as quickly as possible and thus begin delivering large amounts of geothermal power to the Northern California Power Agency per its recent agreement. If the project is delayed past 2011, it will be a bearish sign. At this time the project remains a big question mark. Investors should also monitor whether the Canadian federal government decides to offer tax credits to the geothermal industry for the exploration of geothermal sites. If it does, Western Geopower will be a prime beneficiary.

CONCLUSION Neutral. As a smaller company, Western Geopower is a risky investment. Its focus on the California market makes sense because so many utilities in the state are currently clamoring for renewable energy (in order to meet the renewable energy mandate), but its future success depends on whether the South Meager facility is viable. If it is, Western Geopower is good investment. If not, the investors who are funding the exploration of the site will be left bearing the cost.

Fuel Cells: A Marathon, Not a Sprint

"When you look at the market, you'll see quite a few fuel cell developers are not profitable."
—Sara Bradford, Frost & Sullivan

More seasoned investors might also be surprised to see fuel cells classified as an "alternative" alternative energy—especially since fuel cell technology has been hyped as the next big thing in energy circles since the turn of the century, and prognostications of the coming hydrogen economy have been the subject of numerous books and articles.

In spite of all of this attention, and predictions such as Cleantech Ventures Networks' estimate that the fuel cell industry will grow from $1.4 billion to more than $16 billion by 2015, fuel cells will likely remain a niche technology for at least the next decade. Such a time frame puts it beyond the purview of most investors.

Unlike some analysts who predict that fuel cell technology will *never* take off, my perspective is that it is a very promising technology, but it will just take longer to mature than most of its proponents estimate.

A useful analogy is the creation of hybrid automotive technology. Research into the field began over thirty years ago, but Toyota didn't begin developing its first hybrid vehicle, the Prius, until 1993. Even then, the car itself didn't make it into full-scale production until 1997, and more than a decade later it still represents less than 3 percent of all the vehicles Toyota sells.

Fuel cell technology is not, however, limited to automotive applications. Such cells can also be used as a distributed energy source for large facilities; a backup power source for wireless telecommunications systems in remote areas across the globe;

they can power heavy duty vehicles such as forklifts; and they can even be used as a portable power sources for handheld devices.

Regardless of the application, fuel cells—which generate electricity through an electrochemical conversion process—face a number of obstacles that will need to be addressed before they begin gaining widespread acceptance in the commercial marketplace.

For starters, there is the issue of storage. Storing hydrogen is a difficult issue. In its gaseous state it requires large, high-pressure cylinders, and in its liquid state it must be supercooled to temperatures of minus 250 degrees Celsius. Whether the device is used to power a car, operate a backup power system for a telecommunication company, or power a laptop computer, a convenient and cost-effective storage material will need to be developed first.

Another serious obstacle is the lack of an infrastructure system for delivering hydrogen. The issue is less serious for those fuel cells being used as distributed energy sources to power hospitals and other commercial operations, but it is a serious one for automotive applications.

To understand the problem, it is helpful to know that even if General Motors and other car manufacturers do create an efficient and cost-effective fuel cell, there are only 150 gas stations in the entire country currently capable of providing hydrogen. This compares with 170,000 stations that provide gas. Over time, many of these stations can be upgraded to supply hydrogen, but at a cost of $1 million per facility, such a transition is likely to take some time. (Although it is possible that fuel cells could find a home in powering the fleet vehicles of such large companies or possibly even in some niche applications such as forklifts, locomotives, or marine-based applications.)

The final issue is cost. At the present time, producing hydrogen is still a relatively expensive proposition, consisting of isolating hydrogen from natural compounds—be it water, natural gas, biomass, or coal. The dream, of course, is to create a clean, low-cost method of generating electricity (say from wind or solar power) and then use that electricity to electrolyze water and separate the hydrogen atoms from the oxygen atoms. Unfortunately, such technology is not yet ready for prime time, but it is getting better.

In 2007, for example, Ballard's average cost per kilowatt was $2,800. By 2008, it had dropped to $2,400, and in 2009 it is expected to decrease another 10 percent. Another breakthrough that could dramatically alter the economics of fuel cell technology is the creation of a less expensive catalyst. Researchers are reportedly getting closer to this elusive goal, but they are a long way off from commercial production.

These factors suggest that the development and introduction of fuel cell technology will not be a sprint but rather a marathon. Investors are therefore advised to keep an eye on the field—with special attention being paid to how niche fuel cells application in the areas of backup power systems for military telecommunication facilities and hospitals, as well as powering forklifts, might soon develop. Otherwise it remains too soon to invest in the field with the one possible exception of FuelCell Energy. Having said that, here are a handful of companies that are worth knowing:

Alternative Energy Companies

BLDP	COMPANY	Ballard Power Systems, Inc.
	SYMBOL	BLDP
	TRADING MARKET	NASDAQ
	ADDRESS	9000 Glenylon Parkway, Burnaby, British Columbia, V5J 5J8, Canada
	PHONE	604-454-0900
	CEO	John Sheridan
	WEB	*www.ballard.com*

DESCRIPTION Ballard develops and commercializes proton exchange membrane (PEM) fuel cells and related power generation systems for transportation and stationary applications. It operates in two segments: power generation and materials products.

REASONS TO BE BULLISH

➤ In 2008, Ballard signed a deal with IdaTech to supply the India-based company with 10,000 fuel cells to serve as power generators for wireless telecommunications stations. In 2009, IdaTech confirmed the fuel cells were working properly and will fulfill the entire order—which could be worth as much as $35 million in revenues. It was the largest agreement in Ballard's history and demonstrates that a market for its technology exists.

➤ The company recently sold its automotive fuel cell business to Daimler and Ford. This will allow Ballard to concentrate on more near-term markets such as powering wireless telecommunications stations and the bus industry.

➤ In 2009, Ballard signed a five-year deal with New Flyer, a manufacturer of buses, to complete the construction of twenty heavy-duty fuel cell buses.

REASONS TO BE BEARISH

➤ Ballard has achieved only one year of profitably in its history, and that occurred in 2008 when the $96 million sale of its automotive unit was recorded. Otherwise the company has been a net loser of money and is not expected to achieve profitably until 2011 at the earliest.

continued

Ballard Power Systems continued

➤ With only $60 million cash, at its present burn rate, the company will be forced to go back to the markets in 2011 to raise more money.

WHAT TO WATCH FOR To be successful in the short to midterm, Ballard will need to demonstrate that it can sign other large deals such as the IdaTech agreement. If Ballard can arrange similar deals with wireless telecommunications providers in India, China, and Africa it will be a bullish indicator. Also watch for signs it is penetrating the forklift market. Lastly, you will want to closely monitor the status of governmental support for fuel cell technology. If it wanes, Ballard will be adversely affected.

CONCLUSION Bearish. In spite of the large deal it signed in 2008, Ballard remains a risky proposition. Until the company can line up additional sales and actually become profitable, you would do best to stay away. Fuel cell technology will eventually catch on, but it is unlikely to happen before 2012 and, therefore, the company may need to go back to the public market within the next few years to raise additional capital.

FCEL	COMPANY	FuelCell Energy
	SYMBOL	FCEL
	TRADING MARKET	Nasdaq
	ADDRESS	3 Great Pasture Road, Danbury, CT 06813
	PHONE	203-825-6000
	CEO	Daniel Brdar
	WEB	*www.fuelcellenergy.com*

DESCRIPTION FuelCell Energy is a developer and manufacturer of fuel-cell-based power plants for the commercial, industrial, and utility markets. Its high-temperature systems can generate electricity from natural gas and biomass fuels. The company is also developing both solid oxide fuel cell technology and next-generation carbonate fuel cell and hybrid products.

REASONS TO BE BULLISH

➤ FuelCell's revenues (but not its profits) are growing year to year.

➤ The company is a leading manufacturer of large fuel cell power plants and can scale its systems to supply between 300 KW and 2.4 MW per installation. This makes FuelCell Energy a strong contender to supply large businesses such as hospitals, hotels, and other businesses that have mission-critical energy needs.

➤ Unlike other fuel cells, FuelCell Energy's are scalable for both distributed generation and base load electricity applications.

➤ FuelCell Energy will benefit from both state and federal tax credits. The latter is especially important as its $3,000 per kilowatt credit, together with the eight-year length of the legislation, will dramatically help offset the cost of acquiring and owning fuel cells.

➤ In late 2007, the company received a $131 million order from POSCO, South Korea's leading independent energy provider, for a fuel cell power plant that will eventually generate 68 MW per year.

continued

FuelCell Energy continued

➤ As part of the deal, POSCO also took a 7 percent equity stake in FuelCell Energy, which suggests POSCO likes the company's prospects for future growth.

➤ FuelCell's CEO is a former executive with GE Power Systems, and he also has experience with the Department of Energy. The combination suggests he can navigate the competitive road ahead and understands how to win government contracts.

REASONS TO BE BEARISH

➤ The company has consistently lost money and is not expected to be profitable for the foreseeable future. In 2008, it lost more $93 million, and revenues were off in the first half of 2009.

➤ FuelCell's current cash burn rate is in the neighborhood of $10–20 million per quarter, which suggests it will need to return to the capital market for additional financing in late 2011. If so, this could dilute current shareholder value.

➤ It faces competition from companies such as HydroGen Corporation.

WHAT TO WATCH FOR A big key to the company's long-term success rests with its ability to lower the cost of its fuel cells and increase the stack-life of its cells from three years to five years. Investors will also want to monitor FuelCell's ability to increase the number of multi-MW orders that it makes. The POSCO deal has been a positive development but it will need to make additional such deals. If it can increase annual production to above 100 MW annually, that will be a bullish sign.

CONCLUSION Bullish. The deal with POSCO has played out well for FuelCell, but the company is still not expected to become profitable before 2011. Risk-tolerant investors, however, are encouraged to consider an investment because the stock is now favorably priced and its long-term growth prospects are compelling. It is currently the best pure-play fuel-cell company on the market.

PLUG	COMPANY	Plug Power
	SYMBOL	PLUG
	TRADING MARKET	NASDAQ
	ADDRESS	968 Albany Shaker Road, Latham, NY 12110
	PHONE	518-782-7700
	CEO	Andrew Marsh
	WEB	*www.plugpower.com*

DESCRIPTION Plug Power principally designs, develops, and manufactures proton exchange membrane fuel cell technology for telecommunications, utility, and uninterruptible power supply applications.

REASONS TO BE BULLISH

➤ Plug Power is currently trading at less than the cash and cash-equivalent value of its stock. (Note: Its stock price at time of publication was seventy cents a share, and the company had $144 million cash on hand.)

➤ In 2009, Plug Power is expected to ship 186 of its GenDrive units to Central Grocers, and it received another order for nineteen from the Department of Defense.

➤ The company recently signed a deal with Maxwell Technologies to improve its fuel cells.

REASONS TO BE BEARISH

➤ Plug Power has never made a profit since going public in 1999. During that time it has devoured almost $700. It is expected to burn another $80 million in cash in 2009.

➤ In 2008, the company lost $121 million, and it lost another $8.2 million in the first quarter of 2009 on revenues of only $2.6 million. The company laid off one-third of its workforce in late 2008.

➤ Its major competitor, Ballard Power, has growing sales and a declining burn rate and is doing a better job of securing deals in India's promising telecommunications market.

continued

Plug Power continued

WHAT TO WATCH FOR Plug Power has said that a major milestone for 2010 is to install 1000 GenCore systems. This is an ambitious goal, but if its fuel cells begin to be used in the forklift market, as an energy supply for telecommunications stations in the developing world, or as emergency energy backup for critical government agencies, it is possible the goal could be met.

CONCLUSION Neutral. At eighty cents a share, the company's stock is presently near its all-time low and is selling for less than the company's cash value. If Plug Power can increase its sales, its stock could jump substantially. Plug Power's low price and valuable technology could also make it an attractive take-over target for a larger fuel cell company, which may be willing to pay a premium on its existing stock price. On the downside, Plug Power is still burning cash at a fast rate, and in today's era of tougher credit, it may be difficult for the company to survive beyond 2011.

Don't Catch This Wave Yet . . . the Tide Is Still Out

"I think that most of the 10 to 12 [marine power] companies out there will fall by the wayside."

—Martin Burger, CEO Blue Energy Canada

On its face, marine power—the ability to capture the energy of the ocean's surface waves and tides and convert them into useable electricity—would appear to hold great potential. After all, in addition to being an abundant and fairly reliable energy source that is close to both coastal populations and transmission systems, the technology offers the added benefit of taking up less space than wind farms while creating no visual distractions.

Unfortunately, at this time, it appears that although substantial progress in being made in the area of marine power, the field has not yet approached the stage of development where investors can safely invest in the space. There is only one operational wave power farm in existence. It is located off the coast of Portugal, and in late 2008 it was shut down due to technological and financing problems. While additional wave power parks are under development in England, Scotland, France, and the West Coast of the United States, the industry is unlikely to generate a sizeable amount of energy anytime before 2011—and probably longer.

To this end, in June 2009, Blue Energy Canada received $500 million in financing to pursue the construction of a 200 MW commercial tidal power project. But the company must first construct a 1 MW pilot project and then a 10 MW facility. Only after it has demonstrated these to be viable—a process that is expected to take anywhere between six and nine years—will the full-scale plan proceed.

Still there are two publicly traded companies currently on the market (both of which are profiled) and, by some estimates, another dozen developmental marine power companies, including Verdant, SyncWave, Bourne Energy, Fred Olsen Limited, AWS Ocean Energy, ScotRenewables, Open Hydro, Aquamarine, Wavegen, Tidal Generation, CR Energy, and CleantechCom.

Generally, if you are interested in marine power, I advise you to wait until the technology proves it is truly scalable. Before it can do this it will need to overcome a number of issues. Among the more serious issues confronting the industry is the powerful and destructive nature of the world's oceans. Any successful marine power technology must demonstrate it can, first, withstand the corrosive impact of salt water, and second, handle years of violent storms. Until concerns over the equipment's survivability and reliability can be demonstrated over a considerable period of time, it is unlikely to be considered a viable alternative energy source.

Other issues that will need to be addressed include a variety of regulatory and permit issues. For instance, while most marine power equipment is not visually obtrusive, it is expected to impact marine biology and interfere with commercial fishing interests and shipping lanes. Before large-scale marine powers can be established, such issues will need to be handled to the satisfaction of government regulators, business interests, and public-interest groups.

In many ways, the field of marine power can be likened to the wind power industry of the 1980s. The technology is slowly improving and has immense potential, but it appears that it will be a few years before all the bugs can be worked out and it receives broad governmental approval to begin constructing the type of large-scale wave power or tidal farms that will be necessary to generate the amount of electricity that will capture investors' attention.

FVR	COMPANY	Finavera Renewables
	SYMBOL	FVR
	TRADING MARKET	Toronto Stock Exchange
	ADDRESS	595 Burrard Street, Suite 3113, Three Bentall Centre, Vancouver, British Columbia, Canada V7X 1G4
	PHONE	604-288-9051
	CEO	Jason Bak
	WEB	*www.finavera.com*

DESCRIPTION Finavera Renewables is dedicated to the development of renewable energy resources and technologies with a special focus on wind and wave power technologies. The centerpiece of its wave power portfolio is its patented AquaBuoy wave energy converter. The company is also reportedly in the process of developing various wind power projects in Canada and Ireland.

REASONS TO BE BULLISH

➤ In 2008, the company signed a Power Purchase Agreement with Pacific Gas & Electric.

➤ Finavera has received preliminary regulatory approval from both Washington and California to begin exploring the possibility of locating small wave power projects off the respective coasts of the two states.

REASONS TO BE BEARISH

➤ As of 2009, the company remains a development-phase company and is not generating any revenue. Moreover, it does not have any projects, which suggest that revenue—let alone profits—are nowhere on the near-term horizon.

➤ In 2007 and 2008 it abandoned its wind projects in Germany.

➤ In late 2007, its first AquaBuoy demo project sank off the coast of Oregon.

➤ Finavera faces stiff competition from other wave power start-ups, and investors can expect to see larger companies such as General Electric and Pacific Gas & Electric enter the space.

➤ The company recently raised a small amount of money ($775,000) in the form of a private placement, but it is difficult to see how this funding will do anything more than keep the company afloat through 2010.

WHAT TO WATCH FOR The company's wave power technology appears to be dormant, and its plans to develop wind farms also appear to have stalled. The latter is more likely to actually generate revenue so investors should monitor its ability to secure financing to develop its wind farms.

CONCLUSION Bearish. I strongly advise you to stay away from this stock. It is unlikely its wave power technology will bear fruit, and it is difficult to imagine that in today's climate of tight financing Finavera will receive the necessary capital to develop either its wave power technology or new wind farms.

Alternative Energy Companies

OPTT	COMPANY	Ocean Power Technologies
	SYMBOL	OPTT
	TRADING MARKET	NASDAQ
	ADDRESS	1590 Reed Road, Pennington, NJ 08534
	PHONE	609-730-0400
	CEO	Mark Draper
	WEB	*www.oceanpowertechnologies.com*

DESCRIPTION Started in 1994, Ocean Power Technologies has developed its own proprietary PowerBuoy technology, which captures wave energy using large floating buoys anchored to the seabed. The up and down motion of the device is converted to electrical energy. This power is then transferred via a cable to an onshore transmission system.

REASONS TO BE BULLISH

➤ Ocean Power's technology is currently being investigated for a number of wave power pilot projects around the world.

➤ In early 2009, the company announced it was partnering with Lockheed Martin to develop a utility-scale wave power project in the North America.

➤ In 2008, the company signed a joint development agreement to build a wave power station off the coast of Western Australia. It is expected to produce 10 MW with a potential to expand to 100 MW.

➤ The same year, Ocean Power deployed its PowerBuoy wave energy unit to Iberdrola, a Spanish utility, and signed a $3 million contract to have its wave power systems tested for use by the U.S. Navy.

➤ The fact that wave power uses less space than wind power and isn't burdened by the same aesthetic issues (i.e., unlike wind turbines, wave power system are not readily visible) suggests it could become a formidable competitor to wind power.

REASONS TO BE BEARISH

➤ The company is currently losing money and will likely to continue to do so until its pilot projects are converted into full-scale projects.

➤ Although the company has been testing and improving its technology for more than a decade, the harsh environment of the ocean—especially the corrosive effect of salt water—may prove to be a formidable barrier.

➤ In order to compete effectively, Ocean Power and the entire wave power industry will likely need to depend on government subsidies. If the subsidies aren't renewed, the impact will be significant—and detrimental to investors.

WHAT TO WATCH FOR The key to Ocean Power's success will be to transition its pilot projects into larger operational facilities. Consider it a positive sign if the company deploys enough buoys to produce more than 100 MW of energy. You should also watch for news that the large-scale deal with Lockheed Martin in North America is moving ahead.

CONCLUSION Neutral. While wave power holds great potential, investors are encouraged to think of it like wind power in the 1980s—it will take some time to work the bugs out and for the technology to become cost-competitive with other forms of alternative energy. It may also take a few years before the industry overcomes the skepticism of potential customers, such as large-scale utilities, that wave power is a reliable and affordable form of energy. Nevertheless, of all the wave power companies, Ocean Power Technologies is doing the best job of securing deals, and its partnership with Lockheed Martin suggests it may have access to the financial and technological capital necessary to grow into a profitable company. Investors with a long-term investment horizon and a high tolerance of risk may wish to consider an investment. Ocean Power is the best pure-play investment in the wave power field.

Alternative Energy Companies

COMPANY	Pelamis Wave Power
INVESTORS	Norsk Hydro Technology Ventures, Sustainable Asset Management, Carbon Trust, General Electric, Commons Capital, Merrill Lynch Investment Manager Owners, Emerald Technology Ventures, BlackRock Investment Managers, 3i, and Nettuno Power.
ADDRESS	31 Bath Road, Leith, Edinburgh EH6 7AH, Scotland, UK
PHONE	44-0-131-554-8444
CEO	Phil Metcalf
WEB	*www.pelamiswave.com*

DESCRIPTION Pelamis Wave, formerly known as Ocean Power Delivery, was formed in 1998 and is the developer and manufacturer of the Pelamis system—one of the world's leading wave energy converter technologies. The Pelamis is a semi-submerged structure composed of massive cylindrical sections linked by hinged joints. The wave-induced motion of these joints pumps high-pressure oil through hydraulic motors, which drive electrical generators to produce electricity.

WHY IT IS DISRUPTIVE The company secured its first commercial order for a wave farm back in 2005. The site was being constructed three miles off the coast of Portugal and was expected to generate an estimated 2.25 MW of energy—or enough electricity to power between 1,500 and 15,000 homes. In early 2009, however, the Agucadoura project was called off indefinitely because of leaks in the buoyancy tanks. Nevertheless, the company has recently received an order from E.ON, one of the UK's leading renewable energy generators, and it is currently moving ahead on the development of the Orcadian Wave Farm off the coast of Scotland. The fact that the company was also secured over $40 million from such leading companies as General Electric and Norsk Hydro (a leading European Union energy company) suggests Pelamis' technology has some potential.

WHAT TO WATCH FOR Interested parties should monitor for signs that the company has addressed the technological troubles that plagued the Agucadoura project. Beyond this, it will be imperative that it expands upon Orcadian Wave Farm in Scotland and continues to secure additional deals such as the one with E.ON. If the latter does not encounter problems similar to the Agucadoura wave farm, it will be a positive sign.

CONCLUSION Bearish. Although it is not a publicly traded company, Pelamis appears to be some time away from commercializing a large-scale wave power farm. The fact that it has established relations with leading energy companies suggests that it will be able to line up additional financing and enter into constructive partnerships in the event the projects in Scotland prove successful. Nevertheless, should the company go public, investors would be advised to stay away from the stock until such time as it is actually generating revenues and has a clear path to profitability.

The Black Sheep: Clean Coal

"As president, I will tap our natural gas reserves, invest in clean coal technology, and find ways to safely harness nuclear power."

—President Barack Obama

Because this book is dedicated to environmentally friendly stocks, I debated whether to include profiles of any clean coal companies, since even in its cleanest form coal still emits copious amounts of carbon dioxide.

I opted to provide profiles of two companies engaged in this area for two reasons. First, regardless of one's personal opinion of coal, coal remains the cheapest form of energy currently available (assuming that environmental costs aren't taken into consideration). Second, it is also the most abundant. As such, coal is likely to remain a big part of the global energy picture for at least the next two decades—and perhaps longer. With this in mind, a strong argument can be made that any company engaged in the development of methods or technologies to reduce the amount of harmful greenhouse gases and contaminants from coal, deserves some consideration for being environmentally friendly. Here, then, are two of the more promising clean coal companies:

EEE	COMPANY	Evergreen Energy
	SYMBOL	EEE
	TRADING MARKET	NYSE
	ADDRESS	1225 17th Street, Suite 1300, Denver, CO 80202–5506
	PHONE	303-293-2992
	CEO	Thomas Stoner
	WEB	*www.kfx.com*

DESCRIPTION Evergreen Energy uses a proprietary process to refine abundant, low-grade (sub-bituminous and lignite) coals into a more efficient solid fuel that provides energy with lower emissions. More recently, it formed C-Lock Technologies, a wholly owned subsidiary, which has developed a proprietary counting system for carbon dioxide emissions.

REASONS TO BE BULLISH

➤ Evergreen Energy's K-Fuel technology can reportedly reduce the moisture content of low-grade coal from 30 percent to between 7 and 12 percent. In effect, this increases the coal's heat value from 8,000 Btu per pound to between 10,500 and 11,000 Btu per pound.

➤ U.S. clean air regulations require industrial boilers to limit toxic emissions. Because Evergreen's technology can cut mercury content by up to 70 percent, and sulfur dioxide (SO_2), nitrous oxide (NO_x), and carbon dioxide (CO_2) by measurable amounts, it has an intriguing market opportunity to exploit the situation.

➤ The company's technology does not require users to undergo an extensive or expensive retrofitting.

➤ If the federal government imposes a cap-and-trade system on the management of carbon dioxide, the demand for systems such as C-Lock—which monitors CO_2 emissions—could surge.

➤ To this end, IBM has agreed to help market C-Lock's GreenCert system.

continued

Evergreen Energy continued

REASONS TO BE BEARISH

➤ The company is not yet profitable and, in 2008, reported a loss of $65 million on revenues of only $59 million.
➤ Even in the area of CO2 measurement, Evergreen will face competition from companies such as SAP.

WHAT TO WATCH FOR   The passage of federal legislation regulating carbon emission would be beneficial to Evergreen. Beyond this, news that existing power generating facilities are adopting its technology, as well as indications that the company is making headway in the Asia-Pacific market, would be bullish indicators

CONCLUSION   Bearish. Until legislation that regulates the emission of CO2 is passed and the company is actually profitable, Evergreen remains a risky investment. Investors are encouraged to look elsewhere for growth opportunities.

> **Alternative Energy Companies**

FTEK	COMPANY	Fuel Tech, Inc.
	SYMBOL	FTEK
	TRADING MARKET	NASDAQ
	ADDRESS	27601 Bella Vista Pkwy, Warrenville, IL 60555–1617
	PHONE	630-845-4500
	CEO	John F. Norris
	WEB	*www.ftek.com*

DESCRIPTION Fuel Tech provides engineering solutions for the optimization of combustion systems in utility and industrial applications. It operates two separate segments, Air Pollution Control Reduction Technology and Fuel Chem Technology. The former reduces NOx emissions of flue gas from boilers, incinerators, furnaces, and other combustion sources. The latter uses chemical processes to control a variety of problems in boilers, including slagging, fouling, corrosion, and the formation of sulfur trioxide and carbon dioxide. The company also employs sophisticated software to improve both technologies and processes.

REASONS TO BE BULLISH

➤ Fuel Tech's technology is currently employed in only 400 units worldwide, suggesting that there is a great opportunity for additional growth. By some estimates, three-fourths of the coal plants in the United States don't have the technology to curb NOx emissions, Fuel Tech's technology can help address this problem.

➤ The company's NOx control technology is reported to be able to reduce emissions by 30–85 percent and at a fraction of the cost of competing catalytic technologies.

➤ In spite of coal's many problems, use of this energy source is expected to increase for the foreseeable future. Therefore, efforts to control its harmful emissions are likely to increase.

➤ The growth of coal in China is expected to increase even more rapidly than in the United States, and the market for Fuel Tech's technology could spike as China attempts to limit the smog and pollution caused by NOx emissions.

continued

Fuel Tech, Inc. continued

➤ Fuel Tech's technology was employed by a division of AES in 2009. If successful, it could lead to sizeable follow-on orders.

➤ The company's technology is now being tested in a third Chinese coal plant.

REASONS TO BE BEARISH

➤ In the first half of 2009, both the company's earnings and revenues dropped, and it reported a net loss after a profitable 2008.

➤ While Fuel Tech's technology is cheaper than catalytic technology, the latter is also far more effective. By some estimates catalysts can reduce CO_2 by 90 percent as compared with only a 30 to 80 percent reduction for Fuel Tech's technology.

➤ At the present time, the company only serves a fraction of the market and it faces stiff competition.

➤ Longer term, Fuel Tech will also face competition from other NOx and carbon dioxide controlling technologies such as synthetic genomics.

WHAT TO WATCH FOR Fuel Tech has been testing its technology at three coal plants in China. Since Fuel Tech's future growth depends on some measure of its ability to expand aggressively into this market, investors will want to see progress (in the form of follow-on orders and contract announcements) before investing.

CONCLUSION Bullish. Since 2007, Fuel Tech's stock has experienced a steady erosion. It is now trading 75 percent lower than its high of 2007. If the U.S. government either imposes aggressive environmental regulations, which encourage more coal companies to use Fuel Tech's technology or, alternatively, the China market opens up more than expected, the stock could appreciate considerably. If you have a high tolerance for risk and a long-term investment horizon, Fuel Tech is worth considering.

HW	COMPANY	Headwaters, Inc.
	SYMBOL	HW
	TRADING MARKET	NYSE
	ADDRESS	10653 South River Front Parkway, Suite 300, South Jordan, UT 84095–3529
	PHONE	801-984-9400
	CEO	Kirk A. Benson
	WEB	*www.headwaters.com*

DESCRIPTION Headwaters develops and commercializes technologies to enhance the value of coal, gas, oil, and other natural resources. It also owns Headwaters Technology Group, Inc., a division developing nanocatalysts to convert coal and heavy oils into higher yield, environmentally friendly liquid fuels.

REASONS TO BE BULLISH

➤ Revenues from its clean coal business have increased from $500,000 in 2007 to $13.1 million.

➤ Headwaters' nanocatalyst technology is not currently priced into the stock—it can significantly increase the value chain of coal by helping reduce the amount of NO2 emissions.

➤ The company's fly ash, when mixed in with cement, creates concrete four times stronger and increases its longevity by 100 percent—from twenty-five years to fifty years. As an added benefit, Headwaters' concrete produces less carbon dioxide. If a cap on CO2 is imposed, more builders could begin using its concrete. More important, additional states, such as California, are beginning to mandate the use of fly ash in concrete.

➤ Although this is a longer-term prospect and not related to its alternative energy business, Headwaters is also working to develop a new nanocatalyst that could potentially upgrade heavy oil (of which Canada has a huge reserve) by making it anywhere between 10–20 percent lighter. In 2009, the company entered into a technology alliance with Criterion Catalysts to help refiners use the technology to produce cleaner fuels.

continued

Headwaters, Inc. continued

REASONS TO BE BEARISH

➤ The dramatic slowdown in residential construction seriously hurt the company's revenues and profits in 2008. Revenues were off by 16 percent, and in the first quarter of 2009, the company reported a loss of $406 million (although this included a $465 million goodwill charge).

➤ Nearly 45 percent of Headwaters' revenue comes from its home construction business, and this part of its business took a hit due to 2009's slowing economy and problems in the mortgage market.

➤ The company currently has a debt of more than $500 million.

WHAT TO WATCH FOR If Headwaters' nanocatalyst proves successful in cleaning coal or upgrading heavy oil, it will be a bullish sign. Investors are encouraged to monitor whether coal or oil companies are actively testing this technology.

CONCLUSION Bullish. Headwaters is a contrarian, albeit risky, cleantech investment. The company's investment in clean coal could really pay off, and its HCAT technology offers a great deal of upside. More risk-tolerant investors are encouraged to consider adding it to their portfolio.

Conclusion

All of the aforementioned alternative energies highlighted in this chapter hold great potential, and it is possible all will be successful to varying degrees. When considering an investment in any of technologies, you should keep the following historical analogy in mind.

At the turn of the twentieth century it was by no means apparent that gasoline-powered automobiles would be the chosen technology. As late as 1915, one-third of all automobiles were electric; one-third were steam powered; and one-third ran on gasoline.

For a variety of reasons including cost, convenience, government influence, and technological advancement, gasoline-powered engines won out. The same factors will undoubtedly influence how these emerging energy sources develop. For instance, fuel cell proponents should closely monitor developments in creating membranes and catalysts that more efficiently generate electricity; geothermal advocates are advised to monitor the status of governmental support for the field; marine power supporters should keep a close eye on whether the system can withstand the stress of operating 24/7/365 in the harsh oceanic conditions; and clean coal supporters will have to demonstrate that the energy source can compete in a more environmentally conscious era.

To the extent each field can receive government support and address its individual technological issues, each of the aforementioned energy sources could become more than niche players in tomorrow's clean energy economy.

"The Cleantech Group sees a quadruple bottom-line benefit driving a global focus on energy efficiency in 2009."

—Cleantech Group 2008 Annual Report

Chapter Eight

The Cleanest Form of Energy: Energy Efficiency or Using Less in the First Place

The above quote came from the Cleantech Group's annual list of predictions for the cleantech industry for 2009. The number one prediction was: "Energy efficiency infrastructure boom initiated." No sooner had this prediction been made than General Electric spent $4.3 million to air a thirty-second commercial during the Super Bowl about smart grid infrastructure technology (using the Scarecrow from the *Wizard of Oz* no less). In March, the Obama administration announced that it was spending $4.7 billion on smart grid upgrades as part of the economic stimulus act. Shortly thereafter, the government of China unveiled a massive report entitled "Civil Construction Energy Savings" as part of its annual five-year plan and stated the country intended to cut energy consumption 20 percent by 2012.

In hindsight, neither the Cleantech Group's predictions nor the big plans of the governments of the United States and China or General Electric should have come as a surprise. As I wrote in the 2008 version of this book, "The easiest, cheapest, safest and, ultimately, most effective method of controlling energy costs and its associated environmental issues is to prevent energy from being used in the first place."

From this perspective, a focus on energy efficiency makes a great deal of sense. In fact, a strong argument can be made that it should be the first—if not the primary—area of focus. The benefits are obvious. Energy efficiency can increase profits for both individual consumers as well as businesses by cutting energy costs. Second, from a geopolitical perspective, it reduces demand for imported energy. Third, from a global and environmental perspective, it addresses the need for carbon reduction. And finally, from an economic perspective, it is essential because the demand for energy is outpacing the increase in supply. In other words, if society cannot produce new sources of energy—including from renewable sources—fast enough, people and businesses will have to do with less. They can only do this by using energy more efficiently.

Perhaps not surprisingly, throughout today's energy system there is an extraordinary amount of money just waiting to be saved. For instance, the Federal Regulatory Commission has calculated that American utilities could reduce peak energy demand by as much as 7 percent and, in the process, save $15 billion a year just by deploying smart meter readers and sensors in homes and businesses. The devices could be read by both the consumer and the utility company alike and could control when appliances are operated. By regulating use (or by charging consumers more during high-demand periods), utilities could avoid having to power up additional power plants—which often tend to be older, less efficient coal-powered facilities—in order to meet demand.

At the present time, though, only a fraction (about 6 percent) of all American homes are installed with smart meters. Pacific Gas & Electric is in the process of installing 9.3 million such meters in California, and in Boulder, Colorado, Xcel Energy is building out the first smart grid city. The eventual payoff for both companies could be huge. If the companies can reduce demand by 500 MW it would save the companies the equivalent cost of building one new coal-powered electrical plant. The opportunity is so large that companies as diverse as IBM, Google, Intel, and Microsoft are all now developing technology platforms to address energy efficiency. Comverge and EnerNoc are also moving aggressively to exploit the opportunity.

A related opportunity can be found in the deployment of new sensors through new buildings. These small, relatively low-cost devices (whose price is constantly dropping) can be used to do everything from automatically adjusting the lighting in a room when it isn't being used to providing users the ability to remotely control air conditioners and refrigerators in their homes via the Internet or possibly even their mobile phone. These capabilities are still a few years away from widespread marketplace availability, but they could allow utility companies to shave the peak and reduce consumer energy use when demand is at its highest.

Another piece of low-hanging fruit in today's energy system is lighting. It has been estimated that 30 percent of electrical power generated in the United States is used to power lighting—much of it generated by highly inefficient incandescent light bulbs. (The European Union is scheduled to begin banning traditional incandescent bulbs beginning in 2010.) Wal-Mart, General Electric, and others are now actively engaged in the process of educating U.S. consumers about the extraordinary economic and environmental benefits of switching to the newer compact fluorescent light bulbs (CFLs).

It has so far been a tough sell, primarily because the bulbs are six to eight times as expensive as regular light bulbs. The upside is that the bulbs use 80 percent less electricity and last up to 12,000 hours (as compared to 1,000 hours for an average incandescent light bulb). This means that the bulbs pay for themselves in as little as six months. Over the lifetime of that bulb, the savings amount to $38 per bulb.

More significantly, if every one of America's 110 million households swapped out just one incandescent bulb for a CFL bulb, the country would save enough electricity to power 1.5 million homes or the equivalent of needing to build three new 500 MW coal-powered plants.

The opportunity does not stop there, however. Beyond CFL lighting, other companies, including Philips and Cree, are developing light-emitting diodes (LEDs) that are even more energy efficient and whose positive impact on the environment could be dramatic if the technology gains widespread consumer acceptance.

The final field that appears poised for extraordinary advances in the years ahead in the area of energy conservation is better battery technology. Toyota, Honda, and others have made impressive gains in hybrid automotive technology over the past few years, but so far no truly groundbreaking advances have occurred. This could be about to change. Companies such as A123 Systems, EEStor, and Altair Nanotechnologies are all developing new lithium-ion batteries that can charge faster and hold their power longer. Considering that one-third of all carbon dioxide emissions being emitted into the environment are attributable to automobiles—and considering that the demand for cars in the United States (which is responsible for 45 percent of all automotive emissions), as well as in such countries as China and India, shows no signs of abating—the impact of better battery technology on the environment could be immense.

What follows in this chapter are profiles of a handful of cleantech companies that are trying to make money and help clean the environment by helping people and businesses use new technologies to cut down on fossil fuels.

AONE	COMPANY	A123 Systems
	SYMBOL	AONE
	TRADING MARKET	NASDAQ
	ADDRESS	The Arsenal on the Charles, One Kingsbury Ave, Watertown, MA 02472
	PHONE	617-778-5700
	CEO	David Vieau
	WEB	*www.a123systems.com*

DESCRIPTION A123 is a developer of a new generation of lithium-ion batteries for variety of applications, including power tools, hybrid electric vehicles, home appliances, robotics, and medical devices. The company's proprietary nanoscale electrode technology is purported to give batteries a life ten times longer than ordinary batteries, with power gains up to five times regular batteries, and a dramatically faster recharge time. The company went public in September 2009.

REASONS TO BE BULLISH

➤ A123 has received over $400 million in its IPO debut and is positioning itself as leader in next-generation lithium-ion batteries.

➤ It has been successfully selling products into the commercial marketplace for years and now supplies Black and Decker, Proctor & Gamble, Cessna, Delhi, Google, and BAE Systems.

➤ In 2009, the company announced a strategic alliance with Chrysler to supply energy storage systems for the ENVI Electric Vehicle. The same year it also announced an agreement to supply li-ion cells for Shanghai Automotive hybrid vehicles.

➤ A123 Systems recently announced a partnership with NREL to conduct battery research.

➤ The company has received a $250 million tax credit from the state of Michigan to build its manufacturing facility in the state and is seeking an even larger ($1.8 billion) loan guarantee from the federal government.

REASONS TO BE BEARISH

➤ In late 2008, General Motors announced it had selected LG Chem over A123 Systems because it preferred the former's prismatic cells.

➤ In the past year, revenues from the company's main customer, Black and Decker, have decreased, and losses at A123 are increasing.

➤ Sony, Samsung, and Panasonic, as well as other smaller start-ups, including Sahti3 and Boston Power, are also developing lithium-ion battery technology.

➤ The price of A123's battery technology remains high, and unless it drops lower the product is unlikely to compete successfully in the commercial marketplace.

➤ The long-term viability of its major partner in the U.S. automotive market, Chrysler, remains tenuous.

WHAT TO WATCH FOR The most bullish sign for this company will be if Chrysler begins using the company's battery technology in its hybrid vehicles. The market for these vehicles is expected to grow to almost 4 million by 2012.

CONCLUSION Bearish. A123 appears to have the technology, funding, and commercial partnerships to be a leading player in the battery arena, but until it actually begins producing batteries for the automotive market and making a profit the company remains a big risk. In spite of its very successful IPO (which has inflated prices to $20 per share), investors should remain cautious of this stock until the company is generating batteries for the automotive market and those batteries are being purchased at a price and in a quantity that points toward near-term profitability.

Clean Energy Companies

ALTI	COMPANY	Altair Nanotechnologies, Inc.
	SYMBOL	ALTI
	TRADING MARKET	NASDAQ
	ADDRESS	204 Edison Way, Reno, NV 89502
	PHONE	775-858-2500
	CEO	Terry Copeland
	WEB	*www.altairnano.com*

DESCRIPTION Altair describes itself as a manufacturer of unique nanocrystalline materials. The company states that its proprietary nanomaterials have a variety of applications including, most notably, advanced batteries. It claims to have produced a nanostructured lithium titanate material that enables batteries in hybrid automobiles to operate for hundreds of miles on a single charge and that allows the battery to be recharged within ten minutes.

REASONS TO BE BULLISH

➤ Altair has demonstrated some success landing modest contracts from the U.S. government, including a $3.8 million contract from the U.S. Navy and one from AES, a leading energy provider. Both are testing versions of the company's UPS (Uninterrupted Power Supply) systems.

➤ In 2009, Altair agreed to partner with Amperex to accelerate the commercialization of next-generation lithium-titanate batteries.

REASONS TO BE BEARISH

➤ The company has never been profitable and is burning close to $2 million a month. In 2008, it lost $28 million, and its revenues decreased from $9.1 million to $5.7 million. At this rate, Altair will need to return to investors (again) for additional financing as early as 2010.

➤ Past announcements of new products have consistently failed to materialize, and it has yet to sign a major distribution deal with its battery technology.

➤ Altair faces stiff competition from LG Chem, A123 System, and newer and better financed start-ups such as Sahti3 and Boston Power.

WHAT TO WATCH FOR The company's past history has not demonstrated a promising track record of managerial competence. Nor should investors be persuaded by news that the company is being awarded modest government grants. Only announcements that demonstrate Altair is actually receiving real revenue from commercial customers should be accorded any significance. To this end, additional contracts from either AES or the U.S. Navy would be a positive development

CONCLUSION Bearish. You should treat this stock with great caution. Altair has a new CEO who has brought some strategic focus to the company, but given the tough competition it faces from more established competitors in the battery field, Altair appears unlikely to generate the type of revenue that would justify an investment.

AMSC	COMPANY	American Superconductor Corp.
	SYMBOL	AMSC
	TRADING MARKET	NASDAQ
	ADDRESS	64 Jackson Road, Devens, MA 01434–4020
	PHONE	978-842-3000
	CEO	Dr. Gregory Yurek
	WEB	*www.amsuper.com*

DESCRIPTION   American Superconductor manufactures and sells products using two core technologies, 1) high temperature superconductor (HTS) wires (which are three to five times as efficient at conducting electricity as older cooper wires) and 2) power electric converters that are beneficial in connecting off-grid energy sources such as wind turbines to the electrical grid. The company has also recently begun licensing wind turbine technology.

REASONS TO BE BULLISH

➤ In 2008, revenues grew 63 percent to $180 million, and in the first quarter of 2009 the company reported its first profit of $1.3 million. Revenues and profits are both expected to increase in 2009.

➤ Two macroeconomic trends are working in American Superconductor's favor. First, worldwide demand for electricity will continue to grow, and countries, companies, and customers will need efficient methods for delivering and receiving that electricity. The company's HTS wires can help address this issue. Second, today's existing electricity grid is old, outdated, and vulnerable to blackouts and terrorist attacks. By some estimates the grid will need over $50 billion in investment updates over the coming decade. American Superconductor's technologies could be a big part of this upgrade.

➤ Due to the efficiency of the company's HTS wires, less cable must be used. This lowers installation costs and, more significantly, minimizes environmental siting issues because fewer cables have to be placed across peoples' farms and fewer city sidewalks have to be torn up.

➤ The company signed a deal with Consolidated Edison (the supplier of electricity to New York City) to begin deploying its superconductive power grid technology. As part of the deal, which has been dubbed Project Hydra, the federal government has invested millions. In 2008, the company shipped 17,000 meters of wire to the project.

➤ American Superconductor shipped another 80,000 meters to South Korea for use by the Korea Electric Power Corporation.

➤ American Superconductor's wires also have applications in motors, and the U.S. Navy is testing its high-temperature superconducting system to cloak the magnetic signature of their ships.

➤ In 2008, the company signed a $450 million with Sinoval (China) to license its wind turbine technology and has signed similar, albeit smaller, deals with India, Turkey, and Taiwan.

REASONS TO BE BEARISH

➤ The company is trading at a high price-to-earnings ratio compared to its peers, and it remains subject to the macroeconomic forces.

➤ American Superconductor faces competition from Sumitomo and Zenergy Power in the wire business, and as it grows as a wind power it will face increased competition from that sector's more established players.

WHAT TO WATCH FOR   Investors need to keep a close eye on the status of Project Hydra. If the Secure Super Grid is deployed without problems, it will be a bullish signal and you can expect that other utilities around the nation will begin exploring the possibility of using American Superconductor's technology. Federal legislation helping to offset a portion of the cost of installing new grid technology would also benefit the company substantially. In the area of wind, you should watch for news that more Indian and Chinese companies are licensing the company's technology.

CONCLUSION   Bullish. As stated earlier, a few big trends favor American Superconductor's continued growth: the growing demand for electricity, the need to update today's existing electrical transmission grid, and the developing world's demand for wind power. At the time of publication, the price of its stock is fairly high, but for long-term investors looking for a solid play in the transmission grid—and now increasingly the wind sector—American Superconductor is a strong investment.

COMV	COMPANY	Comverge, Inc.
	SYMBOL	COMV
	TRADING MARKET	NASDAQ
	ADDRESS	120 Eagle Rock Road, East Hanover, NJ 07936
	PHONE	973-884-5970
	CEO	Michael Picchi (Interim)
	WEB	*www.comverge.com*

DESCRIPTION   Comverge provides energy solutions that enhance grid reliability and enable electric utilities to increase available electric capacity during periods of peak demand. Using wireless technology, software, and a sophisticated network of computer processors, the company controls consumers' appliances and reduces electricity consumption during periods of high demand. The benefit is that consumers can cut between 15–25 percent off their monthly electricity bills and utility companies do not need to build new power plants to meet the demand.

REASONS TO BE BULLISH

➤ Comverge increased its revenues by 10 percent in the first quarter of 2009 and brought an additional 450 MW under management in 2008. The company has now installed 5 million devices and counts over 500 utility companies as clients. In total, it controls, operates, and manages 2,600 MW.

➤ Electricity demand is growing at 15–20 percent annually, but supply is only growing at 5 percent. To survive, businesses and homeowners will need to reduce the amount of energy they are using. Comverge's technology helps them achieve this goal.

➤ The $4.7 billion the federal government intends to steer toward smart grid projects could benefit Comverge.

➤ In the past year, the company has signed sizeable deals with Pepco Holding, TransCanada Power, and Arizona Public Service. Each has the potential to generate $100 million in revenue for Comverge over the next fifteen years.

➤ In 2009, the company partnered with Itron to provide real-time communication between utilities and residential customers.

➤ Unlike its other competitors, Comverge counts on residential customers for 25 percent of its business.

REASONS TO BE BEARISH

➤ The company is still not profitable and may not be so for another year or so.

➤ It faces a great deal of competition from companies such as Honeywell, Ener-Noc, and ESCO Technologies.

WHAT TO WATCH FOR   Comverge will face competition from a number of companies. Investors will want to continue to see progress in the amount of MW it has under its control. In 2009, the company expects to add an additional 275 MW. In 2010 and beyond, 500 MW annually is a reasonable goal.

CONCLUSION   Bullish. Ultimately, the cleanest and cheapest source of energy is the energy that never has to be produced. By providing these negawatts to utility companies and by helping customers reduce their energy bill, Comverge is well positioned to grow for the foreseeable future as both consumers and businesses look for ways to control costs. (A *negawatt* is simply a megawatt of energy that never needs to be produced.) The company's stock could really take off if the federal government also begins regulating carbon emissions.

CREE	COMPANY	Cree Inc.
	SYMBOL	CREE
	TRADING MARKET	NASDAQ
	ADDRESS	4600 Silicon Drive, Durham, NC 27703
	PHONE	919-313-5300
	CEO	Charles Swoboda
	WEB	*www.cree.com*

DESCRIPTION   Cree manufactures semiconductor materials and devices, including light-emitting diode (LED) lighting, based on silicon carbide, gallium nitride, silicon, and related compounds. The company's products are used in electronic components (primarily as backlighting), automotive interior lighting, and color electronic displays.

REASONS TO BE BULLISH

➤ Cree is profitable and has an attractive cash flow.

➤ The governments of Canada, California, and the European Union have announced they intend to ban incandescent light bulbs by 2012. These actions should increase the demand for LED lighting.

➤ LEDs face competition from compact fluorescent light (CFL) bulbs, but to date consumer acceptance of CFL bulbs has been slow. This suggests that LED technology might be able to leapfrog CFL technology. Cree estimates its lighting offers an 85 percent energy savings over incandescent bulbs and 50 percent over CFL lighting.

➤ Cree possesses a great deal of experience in silicon carbide and gallium nitride and this experience should help the company improve the quality of its LED lighting as well as lower its cost.

➤ Over the past year, Cree has successfully introduced a number of new programs and has lined up the Pentagon, McDonald's, and numerous universities as customers.

➤ The company has $360 million cash on hand and no long-term debt.

REASONS TO BE BEARISH

➤ In the attractive markets of commercial, industrial, and residential lighting, Cree can expect competition from some large competitors including GE, Siemens, and Philips (which acquired Color Kinetics in 2008).

➤ Cree's LED lights are still more expensive than CFL bulbs and might not be accepted by cost-conscious consumers.

➤ The company is now trading at a lofty price-to-earnings ratio. If sales don't increase significantly in 2010, the stock could experience a decline.

WHAT TO WATCH FOR   Obviously any additional government action banning incandescent lighting (such as the European Union's 2010 ban) will be a boon for Cree. Other federal or state efforts to encourage consumers to purchase more energy efficient lighting would also be beneficial. Long-term investors, however, will want to look for announcements of new LED products and signs that Cree is lowering the price of its products to a level where they are attractive to average household consumers.

CONCLUSION   Bullish. Cree has great potential, as does the entire LED industry. The prospect of further government regulations and incentives suggest that the market for Cree's technology will grow in the near future. The stock is still fairly high priced at this time but, like its one-time competitor Color Kinetics, it remains an attractive acquisition target for larger companies looking to compete with Philips and, like Color Kinetics, could sell at a healthy premium to existing price.

COMPANY	EEStor, Inc.
INVESTORS	Kleiner Perkins Caufield & Byers ZENN Motors
ADDRESS	Cedar Park, TX
PHONE	512-259-5144
CEO	Richard Weir
WEB	*www.eestorbatteries.com*

DESCRIPTION   EEStor is dedicated to designing, developing, and manufacturing high-energy storage devices. The company has developed a ceramic ultracapacitor with a barium-titanate dielectric that generates an enormous amount of energy. The company's stated goal is to "replace the electrochemical battery" in everything from laptop computers and low-end electric vehicles to SUVs and utility-scale electricity storage systems.

WHY IT IS DISRUPTIVE   If the company is to be believed, its technology will be able to produce ten times as much energy as a lead-acid battery at half the cost and without using any toxic materials or chemicals. Under such a scenario, an electric car would be able to travel 500 miles (at speeds of up to 80 miles per hour) on just $9 of electricity. As an added benefit, the device is said to be able to recharge in just a couple of minutes. Obviously, the technology holds the potential to revolutionize the automotive industry. The company has signed exclusive deals with Lockheed Martin to use its Electrical Energy Storage Units (EESU) in military and homeland security applications.

WHAT TO WATCH FOR   In 2009, ZENN motors of Toronto made a sizeable $5 million follow-on investment in the company, and it expects to receive EEStor's EESU for use in its electrical vehicles by the beginning of 2010. If this milestone is met and the technology works as promised, there should be a great deal of publicity surrounding the event because of its implications for the automobile industry. If EEStor announces additional material progress of its batteries (e.g., being able to perform at cold temperatures) or if it can demonstrate it is lowering the cost of its technology, either event will be a bullish indicator. The most important things to watch for, however, are: 1) whether EEStor delivers an actual project to Zenn in early 2010; and 2) whether Zenn then begins marketing and selling those vehicles.

CONCLUSION   The lack of tangible information and the company's secretive nature makes its technology hard to assess. Nevertheless, since Kleiner Perkins and ZENN Motors have both made large investments in EEStor there may be more than just hype behind its technology. In the event the company does go public, if you're looking for a high-risk, high-reward investment, you may want to consider the company. A123, Altairnano, Valence, NEC, and Sony are all developing competing technology.

ENOC	COMPANY	EnerNoc, Inc.
	SYMBOL	ENOC
	TRADING MARKET	NASDAQ
	ADDRESS	75 Federal Street, Suite 300, Boston, MA 02110
	PHONE	617-224-9900
	CEO	Timothy Healy
	WEB	*www.enernoc.com*

DESCRIPTION   EnerNoc provides demand response and energy management solutions to commercial and industrial customers by remotely managing electricity consumption. The company uses a variety of tools, including energy analytics and controls services, to manage over 2,700 MW of electric capacity.

REASONS TO BE BULLISH

➤ EnerNoc can reduce electricity demand by 300 MW within minutes. This type of scale and speed will attract the attention of utilities looking to better manage their power and avoid having to buy energy on the spot market at high prices. In the past year, the company has added nine utility customers, including the Tennessee Valley Authority and Green Mountain Power.

➤ In the past year, the company has become profitable, and its gross margins are now up to 42 percent.

➤ In 2008, EnerNoc acquired eQuilibrium in an attempt to move into the carbon tracking business.

➤ The company's technology can often relieve utilities from having to build a new power plant to meet growing demand (which can be an expensive proposition) or, alternatively, from having to fire up an auxiliary power plant to meet surging demand during peak periods.

➤ Today, utilities are having a difficult time getting siting approval for new transmission lines. EnerNoc's technology can relieve some this pressure by reducing demand.

➤ In the event the federal government imposes carbon restrictions, utilities will benefit immensely from the negawatts EnerNoc can produce.

REASONS TO BE BEARISH
➤ The company faces competition from companies such as Comverge, Honeywell, IBM, and even potentially Google.
➤ Its move into carbon tracking could divert attention from its core business. It will also face competition in this emerging area from SAP and Microsoft.

WHAT TO WATCH FOR   The market for demand response systems is growing and is still in the early stages of its growth. Watch to see if EnerNoc can continue to sign up additional utilities and bring on 500 MW (or more) annually of demand management energy in 2010 and beyond. Also, if the company's international division can begin lining up new customers in foreign markets, especially China, it will be a bullish sign. Longer term, you should monitor whether EnerNoc's move into the carbon tracking business is paying dividends. If so, the synergy of this technology with its core business could prove beneficial in helping EnerNoc win customers from competitors such as Comverge.

CONCLUSION   Bullish. Often, utility companies need to build expensive power plants to keep in reserve in the event their customers need extra energy (such as on hot summer days). The problem is that these plants require an extensive amount of capital but operate for a few days every year. As such they are expensive to maintain. A better solution is to reduce the demand for electricity during these periods. This is what EnerNoc's technology does, and it is likely to become a more important tool for every utility.

Conclusion

The cheapest and cleanest form of energy that any business or person can use is energy that isn't generated in the first place. The idea is simple, and yet it hasn't been fully embraced by either corporations or consumers. This is slowly changing as environmental concerns have raised individual and corporate awareness about their impact on the environment. As noble or well intentioned as these efforts may be, they haven't really translated into action. What really matters is money, and the push toward energy efficiency is largely being driven by its potential to save people money—in many cases lots of money.

For instance, after labor costs, energy is the second largest expense for most retailers. This fact has now caused Wal-Mart to publicly state that it intends to cut energy usage in its stores by 30 percent over the coming decade. On a much larger scale, the government of China believes it can reduce energy consumption by 20 percent in the next five years.

Ultimately, it is this type of attention that will drive new businesses and entrepreneurs alike to find ways to help government, corporations, small business owners, and residential users save money. The end result will likely be an explosion of innovations over the coming years, and the prudent investor stands to profit handsomely by being alert to the companies that are delivering these innovations.

As an individual investor, you would be wise to focus on energy efficiency as an investment theme for two additional reasons. First, as 2008 demonstrated, sectors such as wind, solar, and biofuels can be extremely volatile. Energy efficiency, however, because it is all about reducing costs, is countercyclical. It does not go out of fashion. Secondly, as was explained earlier, it is a matter of simple economics. The demand for energy is outpacing supply. The fastest, easiest, and most economical and environmentally friendly method of addressing this shortcoming is for everyone to use energy more efficiently.

"Renewable energy is proven technology, the price is dropping, the whole world is going that way, that's where our investments should be going."

—Bob Brown

Chapter Nine

Tracking Cleantech and Creating Your Own Cleantech Mutual Fund

It should go without saying that investing can be a risky business. Nevertheless, I feel compelled to offer yet another warning that investing in cleantech will likely be more volatile than investing in other more traditional sectors. The reasons for this have been spelled out in the preceding pages but bear repeating. For starters, every renewable energy source is competing against the larger and more established energy sources such as oil and gas, natural gas, coal, and nuclear power. In most cases these sources are still cheaper than renewable energy sources and will likely remain so for the near-term future. Furthermore, these industries also have powerful political constituencies, and to the degree that renewable energy must continue to rely on generous government subsidies, these vested interest groups could lobby vociferously against the continuation of government subsidies for clean energy. This is especially true as concerns over the impact of the economic stimulus package on the federal budget deficit become more pronounced.

A second concern is that different renewable energy sources will also be competing directly with one another. For example, certain homeowners may be inclined to install either a solar module on their roof or a wind turbine in their backyard but, for cost considerations, will not do both. Which system they choose will be determined by a combination of factors including upfront installment costs, the amount and reliability of the power that the system can be expected to generate, expected payback time, ease of use, aesthetic issues, local zoning regulations, and, of course, the availability of tax credits. Such concerns will also affect how businesses, governments, utilities, and possibly even entire communities will select between various renewable energy options. The bottom line is that depending on the amount of technological progress made in the different fields, certain alternative energy sources can be expected to be either more or less competitive than others.

There is also the issue of intra-industry competitiveness. The debates between biofuels and synthetic biofuels; silicon solar cells and thin-film cells; or which wind turbine manufacturer can produce the largest, most efficient turbine are legitimate concerns and have not been adequately settled yet—and won't be for some time. Again, it is worth reiterating that the development of new manufacturing methods, new technological breakthroughs, and the availability of government subsidies could tip the scale in favor of one type of renewable energy virtually overnight.

For all of these reasons, it is imperative that you stay abreast of advances in the field. Many will be covered in the leading financial newspapers such as the *Wall Street Journal*, *Barron's*, and *The Economist*, but active investors are encouraged to add a few additional sources to their daily reading list.

Informative websites and blogs that will keep you aware of the latest activity include:

Renewable & Alternative Energy News: *www.terrawatts .com/current.html*. The site offers a solid compilation of industry news gleaned from a variety of news sources around the world. For readers looking for a quick, one-stop site for the latest news about the renewable energy sector, it does an excellent job of covering the major stories.

Greentechmedia: *www.greentechment.com*. Another superb site on cleantech, this website covers every renewable energy sector and offers extensive coverage on the smaller fields such as wave power and geothermal energy. Frequently, the site will be the first to break news and, on occasion, offer live coverage of conferences and symposia that delve in greater detail about some of the more complex and technical aspects of clean technology. Its lead journalist, Michael Kanellos, does a thorough job of tracking technological advances and its main blogger, Rob Day, keeps readers apprised of the latest news from the cleantech venture capital community. The site also contains a useful search engine that can be used by investors to research individual businesses involved in cleantech.

Cleantech.com: *http://cleantech.com*. Sponsored by the Cleantech Group, a leading research organization in the field, the website offers daily articles on virtually every aspect of clean technology. It is an invaluable tool for investors wishing to stay atop the latest industry news, technological breakthroughs, and venture capital deals. For active investors it also offers a premium paid website that offers market research and exclusive interviews and articles.

The one thing that these news sources, websites, and blogs do not do in great detail is evaluate the more complex issues that are important in determining a company's prospects. Here I am speaking of assessing a company's management skills, financial strength, marketing prowess, or the strength of its intellectual property. (These are issues, I might add, that often elude the most seasoned and dedicated of investing experts.)

These issues, in combination with the previously mentioned risks (e.g., competing against traditional energy suppliers, the threats posed by new technological developments, etc.) cause a number of investors to ask the very logical question of whether there are mutual funds or exchange traded funds covering the cleantech space.

Luckily, the answer is "yes," and for investors who don't have the time or patience to research and stay abreast of the scores of publicly traded cleantech companies, investing in one of these funds is a prudent way to gain exposure to a diversified mix of cleantech companies. As with individual stocks, you should do your due diligence on these funds before investing in any one. Pay special attention to the philosophical approach of each fund, and monitor the filters that they use for selecting those companies that will compose their portfolios. Often, you may find that these funds' interests are different than your own. Also pay close attention to the load charges and annual expense rates that accompany each fund.

With those caveats, here then are some of the leading cleantech funds:

PowerShares WilderHill Clean Energy Portfolio

This exchange traded fund (ETF), created in 2005, was the first alternative energy ETF and trades under the symbol "PBW" on the American Stock Exchange. By focusing on "greener and generally renewable sources of energy and technologies that facilitate cleaner energy," the fund closely aligns with the term *cleantech* as defined by this book and has a low (0.6 percent) annual expense ratio. On the downside, the fund skews heavily toward solar—especially Chinese—solar stocks and avoids wind stocks altogether. It is designed to replicate the growth and appreciation of the WilderHill Clean Energy Index.

As of July 2009, the fund's top holdings were:

- ➤ Broadwind Energy (3.53 percent)
- ➤ Trina Solar (2.94 percent)
- ➤ Applied Material (2.93 percent)
- ➤ Universal Display (2.79 percent)
- ➤ Echelon Corp. (2.78 percent)
- ➤ Evergreen Solar (2.7 percent)
- ➤ JA Solar (2.63 percent)
- ➤ Ormat Technologies (2.62 percent)
- ➤ First Solar (2.55 percent)
- ➤ Yingli Green Energy (2.49 percent)
- ➤ American Superconductor (2.48 percent)
- ➤ FuelCell Energy (2.40 percent)

Van Eck Global Alternative Energy ETF

Another exchange traded fund, this one trades under the symbol "GEX" on the New York Stock Exchange and seeks to provide targeted exposure to companies that are engaged in the alternative energy industry. Its top ten holdings as of July 2007 include:

➤ Vestas Wind System (18.46 percent)
➤ First Solar (9.2 percent)
➤ MEMC (6.24 percent)
➤ Iberdrola Renovables (5.73 percent)
➤ Gamesa Corp. (5.71 percent)
➤ Kurita Water (5.54 percent)
➤ Verbund AG (4.94 percent)
➤ Cree (3.78 percent)
➤ Covanta Holdings (3.67 percent)
➤ EDP (3.45 percent)

This fund was launched in 2007, and like PowerShares WilderHill it has a relative low (0.65 percent) annual fee. Note as of late 2009 it is more heavily invested in wind power (Vestas and Gamesa) than some other funds and has more exposure to global companies than other mutual funds and ETFs. The fund also has a screen that blocks from its portfolio companies that generate less than 70 percent of their revenues from alternative energy. This precludes larger and more diversified companies such as General Electric and Siemens from being included in the fund. (Of the ETFs and mutual funds listed, this is my favorite.)

New Alternative Fund

A mutual fund that trades under the symbol "NALFX." This fund, which was started in 1982, has the honor of being the oldest alternative energy mutual fund in existence. The fund's top ten holdings include:

- ➤ EDF (5.36 percent)
- ➤ EDP Renovaveis (5.24 percent)
- ➤ Acciona SA (5.19 percent)
- ➤ Iberdrola Renovables (5.16 percent)
- ➤ Abengoa SA (5.13 percent)
- ➤ Schneider Electric (5.03 percent)
- ➤ American Water Works (4.94 percent)
- ➤ Basic Sanitation Company of the State of Sao Paulo (4.70 percent)
- ➤ Vestas Wind Systems (4.55 percent)
- ➤ Atmos Energy Corporation (4.51 percent)

The advantage of this mutual fund is its lengthy track record. The disadvantage is that the fund has a 4.75 percent load and an annual expense ratio of 0.95 percent. It also has a slightly different screen for the stocks that it selects. It tends to look at other social factors in addition to renewable energy. As such, the fund includes a number of stocks that are not covered in this book.

Guinness Atkinson Alternative Energy Fund

This mutual fund trades under the symbol "GAAEX" on Nasdaq and, like the other funds, has holdings in companies involved in alternative energy. Its top ten holdings are:

- ➤ JA Solar (3.85 percent)
- ➤ Hansen Transmission (3.74 percent)
- ➤ EDF Energies (3.64 percent)

➤ Wacker Chemie (3.56 percent)
➤ Suntech Power (3.56 percent)
➤ Verbund (3.51 percent)
➤ EDP Renovaveis (3.39 percent)
➤ Novera Energy (3.38 percent)
➤ SMA Solar Technologies (3.35 percent)
➤ Vestas Wind Systems (3.31 percent)

The fund was initiated in 2006 and has since lost 17 percent annually. In part, this is because of the global recession and because the fund invests in smaller, high-growth foreign companies. I do not recommend this fund because it does not attempt to maintain a diversified portfolio and it has a very high expense ratio (1.98 percent).

For investors interested in funds with a more specific focus and lower costs, the following are worth considering:

Claymore/Mac Global Solar Index ETF (symbol TAN) focuses on global solar companies.
First Trust Global Wind Energy Index (symbol FAN) focuses on global wind companies.

Building Your Own Fund

If none of these funds appeal to you, the option always exists to create your own customized cleantech fund. However, because every investor has a different set of objectives for investing, and each investor has his or her own tolerance for risk, the purpose of this section is not to design a one-size-fits-all cleantech mutual fund (although I offer a model portfolio). Rather, it is to provide you with a prudent method for approaching investing in this field.

To begin, almost every financial advisor urges clients to diversify their portfolios with a mix of bonds, stocks, and some cash. More cautious investors or those who have a shorter investment horizon are encouraged to carry a heavier mix of bonds. Those who are more aggressive or who have a longer time before retirement typically invest more in equities. (I will leave it to you to determine how much of your portfolio, if any, you wish to invest in bonds.)

The next consideration is to diversify your stock portfolio across a variety of industrial sectors. The logic is simple. Due to the cyclical nature of many sectors, it is unwise to invest too much in any one sector on the chance that it experiences a downswing and drags down your overall portfolio performance with it.

The same logic applies to finding an appropriate balance between U.S. and foreign stocks. Political events, fluctuations in currency valuations, and a host of other economic factors can hit any one market particularly hard, and having a well-balanced portfolio helps hedge against such factors.

Be wary of investing too high of a percentage of your portfolio in cleantech stocks. Again, it is a personal decision but prudence would dictate that an appropriate level would be around 5 and 10 percent—with the remainder split up among various other sectors including health care, financial services, materials/chemicals, and bonds. There is, of course, some flexibility especially if a portion of your cleantech portfolio includes some of the larger companies—such as those mentioned in Chapter 3—which provide additional exposure to different markets.

As for investing in foreign stocks, this makes sense for the sake of diversification and because some of the most promising cleantech companies are located in China, Denmark, and Germany.

The next consideration is to determine how to divide up your cleantech portfolio between large companies and small and medium-sized businesses. As a general rule, large cap stocks (over $1 billion in annual revenues) demonstrate less volatility, whereas small and mid-cap stocks are more prone to larger deviations.

Lastly, most financial advisors encourage you to keep a certain amount of cash on hand in order to meet large unexpected expenses and to hedge against unforeseen life events—like sudden unemployment. Again, it is a prudent strategy, but for our purposes, I am going to suggest you keep a small amount of cash on hand in the event a promising cleantech company files for an initial public offering (IPO)—something that is likely to happen a fair amount over the coming years.

With all of these factors in mind, I therefore encourage cleantech investors to determine their own mix among these various categories: foreign and U.S. stocks, large and small cap stocks, and the various cleantech sectors: biofuels, wind, solar, energy efficiency, and a catch-all category labeled *miscellaneous*, which captures some of those companies that represent more aggressive innovative cleantech plays or are, alternatively, pursuing one of the smaller niche clean technologies such as wave power.

The following is a suggested portfolio for a typical forty-year-old investor wishing to pursue a moderately aggressive investment strategy in clean technology

	Large Cap	Mid Cap	Small Cap
	35 percent	30 percent	25 percent
Solar (25 percent)	First Solar	SunTech Power	Trina Solar
Wind (25 percent)	GE	Vestas	Clipper Windpower
Energy Eff. (20 percent)	IBM	Amer. Superconductor	Comverge
Biofuels (10 percent)	ADM	The Anderson's	Metabolix
Misc (10 percent)	Google	Ormat	FuelCell Energy
Cash (10 percent)			

As for the remaining 10 percent, I recommend keeping it in cash in the event a private company such as Synthetic Genomics, HelioVolt, Miasole, Nanosolar, or Konarka goes public.

The odds are that some of them will return spectacular gains in the years ahead.

Conclusion

In some ways investing in the stock market is comparable to life on the African Savannah. That is to say, to survive and prosper it is essential to first avoid being slaughtered. Next, one must then be smart enough, fast enough, or lucky enough to be able find someone else to prey upon.

The analogy, of course, isn't perfect, but I would encourage you to keep the African Savanna in mind in the years ahead as you seek to navigate the bountiful, yet treacherous, fields of green investing. Think about how some animals survive on the savanna by working in partnership with other animals.

One of the better-known examples is the unusual affiliation among wildebeests, zebras, and ostriches. Alone each species is vulnerable. Together, however, this triumvirate forms an impressive survival team. The wildebeest has very good hearing but poor eyesight and sense of smell. Zebras, on the other hand, have only modest hearing and eyesight but are endowed with a keen sense of smell, while ostriches possess excellent eyesight. By relying on the relative strengths of the other animals, the trio can often detect predators well in advance and take the necessary precautions to keep the threat at bay. As such, they can also survive a long time and reach their destination.

In the same way, investing is a long-term game, and reaching one's final destination—presumably a comfortable retirement—is the goal. To survive, diversity is an integral survival technique. This is especially true with regard to cleantech investing. As the eighty-five+ profiles in this book testify, there is no shortage of exciting opportunities in the field.

Some investors may be inclined to put all their money in one particular sector or, worse, just one or two select stocks. I would strongly advise against such a strategy. At this stage of cleantech development, it is impossible to know not only which alternative energy source will do the best but which company (or companies) within that sector will represent the best growth opportunities.

The best way to survive and prosper is to load up your cleantech portfolio with a healthy mix of solar, biofuel, energy efficiency, and wind companies. You may even want to add a fuel cell company, a geothermal company, or a wave power company to the mix.

The bottom line is that there is no shortage of clean and abundant energy—be it in the form of sunlight striking the earth, winds blowing through the skies, the tides moving the oceans, biomass growing from the fields, or heat pulsating below the earth's surface. The proverbial "$64 billion question" remains which source or sources can convert that energy most efficiently? My opinion is that it will be a combination of these sources and that it therefore makes sense to have companies in each field in one's portfolio. In other words, don't think that a single silver bullet will return a prize trophy. You are better off approaching the green energy opportunity with silver buckshot.

INDEX